GCSE OCR Gateway

Additional Science

Higher Workbook

This book is for anyone doing **GCSE OCR Gateway Additional Science** at higher level.
It covers everything you'll need for your year 11 exams.

It's full of **tricky questions**... each one designed to make you **sweat**
— because that's the only way you'll get any **better**.

There are questions to see **what facts** you know. There are questions
to see how well you can **apply those facts**. And there are questions
to see what you know about **how science works**.

It's also got some daft bits in to try and make the whole
experience at least vaguely entertaining for you.

What CGP is all about

Our sole aim here at CGP is to produce the highest
quality books — carefully written, immaculately presented
and dangerously close to being funny.

Then we work our socks off to get them
out to you — at the cheapest possible prices.

Contents

MODULE B4 — IT'S A GREEN WORLD

MODULE C4 — THE PERIODIC TABLE

MODULE P4 — RADIATION FOR LIFE

Published by CGP

Editors:
Katie Braid, Emma Elder, Mary Falkner, David Hickinson, Edmund Robinson, Helen Ronan, Lyn Setchell, Hayley Thompson, Jane Towle, Julie Wakeling, Dawn Wright.

Contributors:
Michael Aicken, Steve Coggins, Mike Dagless, Ian H Davis, James Foster, Paddy Gannon, Dr Giles R Greenway, Dr Iona M J Hamilton, Derek Harvey, John Myers, Andy Rankin, Claire Ruthven, Sidney Stringer Community School, Paul Warren.

ISBN: 978 1 84762 757 5

With thanks to Janet Cruse-Sawyer, Chris Elliss, Ben Fletcher, Ian Francis and Karen Wells for the proofreading.

With thanks to Jan Greenway, Laura Jakubowski and Laura Stoney for the copyright research.

Data used to draw graph on page 11 developed by the National Center for Health Statistics in collaboration with the National Center for Chronic Disease Prevention and Health Promotion (2000). http://www.cdc.gov/growthcharts

Groovy website: www.cgpbooks.co.uk

Printed by Elanders Ltd, Newcastle upon Tyne.
Jolly bits of clipart from CorelDRAW®
Based on the classic CGP style created by Richard Parsons.

Cells

Q1 **Bacterial cells** are different from **plant** and **animal cells**.

a) Tick the boxes to show whether the following statements apply to plant, animal or bacterial cells. Some of the statements apply to more than one type of cell.

	Bacterial Cells	Plant Cells	Animal Cells
i) A nucleus is present.	☐	☐	☐
ii) Contains a single circular strand of DNA.	☐	☐	☐
iii) DNA is arranged in chromosomes.	☐	☐	☐

b) Name two features of a typical plant cell that aren't seen in bacterial cells.

1. ....

2. ....

Q2 Ibrahim uses a light microscope to look at a **liver cell**. The diagram below shows what he can see.

a) i) Explain why the liver cell has so many mitochondria.

....

....

ii) Name **one** other type of cell that contains a large number of mitochondria.

....

b) Ibrahim uses his light microscope to look for **ribosomes** in the cell.

i) Explain why Ibrahim can't see any ribosomes.

....

ii) In what part of the cell are ribosomes found?

....

iii) Name the cell process which takes place at the ribosomes.

....

2

DNA

Q1   Choose from the words below to complete the passage about the **structure** of DNA.

> U   bases   A   helix   chromosomes
> protein   G   B   cross   genes   complementary

.... are long, coiled molecules of DNA divided into short sections called

.... DNA is a double-stranded .... made up of four

different .... — these are ...., C, ... and T.

The two DNA strands are joined together by .... links, which form

between .... base-pairs.

Q2   Complete the diagram below to show which **bases** will form the complementary strand of DNA.

A	C	T	G	C	A	A	T	G
.....	.....	.....	.....	.....	.....	.....	.....	.....

Q3   Number the statements below to show the correct order of the stages in **DNA replication**.

☐ Cross links form between the bases and the nucleotides are joined together.

☐ Two double-stranded molecules of DNA are formed.

☐ The DNA double helix 'unzips' to form two single strands.

☐ Bases on free-floating nucleotides pair up with complementary bases on the DNA.

Q4   A **model** of DNA was first developed by two scientists called Watson and Crick. They used data that had been collected by other scientists.

a) i) Tick the box next to the statement below that correctly describes some of the data they used.

1.   X-ray data showing there was a single chain of DNA wound in a helix. ☐

2.   X-ray data showing there were two chains of DNA wound in a helix. ☐

3.   Infra-red data showing there were two chains of DNA wound in a helix. ☐

ii) What other data did Watson and Crick use to develop their model?

....

b) Suggest why new discoveries like Watson and Crick's are not always immediately accepted.

....

....

**Protein Synthesis**

Q1   Circle the correct words in the pairs to complete the sentences below.

a)   A gene is a section of DNA that codes for a **particular protein** / **cell structure**.

b)   Each gene contains **a different** / **the same** sequence of bases.

c)   Proteins are made up of chains of **amino acids** / **glucose**.

d)   Each amino acid is coded for by a sequence of **three** / **four** bases.

Q2   Choose from the words below to complete the passage about **cell function**.

| on | full set | off | enzymes |
| functions | | divides | amino acids |

The proteins produced by a cell determine how it .... For example,

cell reactions are controlled by proteins called .... Every cell contains

a .... of genes, but some of these genes are switched ....

— this means that the proteins they code for can't be made. As a result, only the genes

that are switched .... determine the function of the cell.

Q3   DNA controls the production of **proteins**.

a)   How do **amino acids** determine the function of a protein?

    ....

b)   How is the **sequence** of amino acids determined?

    ....

Q4   **mRNA** is a copy of the code in DNA.

a)   Describe the role of mRNA in the production of proteins.

    ....

    ....

b)   Explain why a **copy** of the DNA code is needed to make proteins.

    ....

    ....

4

Functions of Proteins

Q1 Draw lines to match each **protein** to its type and function.

protein	type	function
insulin	structural protein	transports oxygen around the body
haemoglobin	hormone	strengthens connective tissues
collagen	carrier molecule	regulates blood sugar level

Q2 a) Tick the boxes to show whether the sentences are **true** or **false**.

True False

   i) Enzymes slow down chemical reactions in living cells. ☐ ☐

   ii) The reactions involved in photosynthesis are controlled by enzymes. ☐ ☐

   iii) Enzymes don't control reactions involved with protein synthesis. ☐ ☐

b) Write a correct version of each false sentence in the space below.

....

....

Q3 Enzymes are **biological catalysts**. They have a **high specificity** for their substrate.

a) What is a **catalyst**?

....

b) i) What does it mean when enzymes are described as having '**high specificity**'?

....

   ii) Explain why enzymes have a high specificity for their substrate using the term '**lock and key mechanism**'.

....

....

c) In the space provided, draw a labelled diagram to show how an enzyme's shape allows it to break substances down.

More on Enzymes

Q1 This graph shows the results from an investigation into the effect of **temperature** on the rate of an **enzyme-catalysed** reaction.

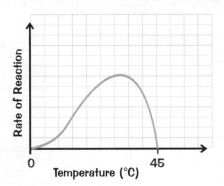

I'm melting, melting. What a world, what a cruel, cruel world.

enzyme

a) What is the **optimum** temperature for this enzyme?

....

b) Explain why the rate of an enzyme-catalysed reaction is **slow** at **low temperatures**.

....

....

c) Describe what happens to an enzyme at temperatures **above** its optimum and give the technical term for this.

....

....

Q2 Professor Cuten wants to calculate the Q_{10} value of an enzyme-catalysed reaction. The **rate of reaction** at different temperatures is shown in the table below.

Temperature (°C)	Rate of Reaction (cm³/s)
10	2
20	6
30	18
40	54
50	162

a) What does a Q_{10} value show?

....

....

$$Q_{10} = \frac{\text{rate at higher temperature}}{\text{rate at lower temperature}}$$

b) **i)** Using the formula in the box above calculate the Q_{10} value of the reaction.

....

ii) What does this Q_{10} value tell you about the rate of the reaction?

....

More on Enzymes

Q3 Stuart has a sample of an enzyme and he is trying to find out what its **optimum pH** is. Stuart tests the enzyme by **timing** how long it takes to break down a substance at different pH levels. The results of Stuart's experiment are shown in the table below.

pH	time taken for reaction in seconds
2	101
4	83
6	17
8	76
10	99
12	102

a) On the grid below draw a line graph of the results of the experiment.

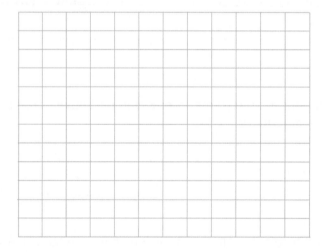

b) What is the **optimum** pH for the enzyme?

....

c) Explain why the reaction is very slow at certain pH levels.

....

....

d) Would you expect to find this enzyme in the stomach? Explain your answer.

....

Remember, the pH in the stomach is very low.

e) Describe **two** things that Stuart could do to make sure his experiment is a fair test.

1. ....

2. ....

Mutations

Q1 a) Tick the correct boxes to show whether the following statements are **true** or **false**.

                                                                True False

  i) Mutations are always harmful.   ☐   ☐

  ii) Mutations can occur spontaneously.   ☐   ☐

  iii) Mutations can prevent the production of a protein.   ☐   ☐

  iv) Mutations never lead to the production of different proteins. ☐ ☐

  v) Mutations are changes to the cell cytoplasm.   ☐   ☐

  vi) Mutations sometimes have no effect.   ☐   ☐

Ben's pet ant had been mute since the unfortunate squishing incident.

b) Write a correct version of each false sentence in the space below.

....

....

....

Q2 Suggest explanations for the following facts.

a) In 1986, a nuclear reactor at Chernobyl in the Ukraine exploded. Afterwards, the rate of thyroid cancer amongst children in the surrounding region increased by approximately 1000%.

....

....

b) Smokers are more likely to suffer from lung cancer than non-smokers.

....

....

Q3 Suggest how some mutations might be **beneficial**.

....

....

....

Top Tips: Sadly mutations in the real world are nowhere near as awesome as the ones in films and comics — no mutation has ever given anyone x-ray vision, telepathy or the ability to fly. Make sure you know how mutations are caused and the sorts of results they really have.

Module B3 — Living and Growing

Multiplying Cells

Q1 **Mitosis** is a type of cell division.

What does mitosis produce cells for?

....

....

How did you say you
wanted the cell dividing?

Q2 Complete the passage using the words provided below.

divide	centre	replicated	opposite	line up

Before mitosis starts, the DNA in a cell is ....

At the beginning of mitosis, the DNA coils into double-armed chromosomes

that .... along the .... of the cell.

The chromosomes then .... as the cell fibres pull them apart.

The two arms of each chromosome move to .... poles of the cell.

Q3 Many creatures have evolved to be **multicellular**.

a) Explain two advantages of being **multicellular** compared to being **single-celled**.

1. ....

....

2. ....

....

b) Suggest why multicellular organisms need the following specialised organ systems:

i) a nervous system

....

ii) a respiratory system

....

iii) a circulatory system

....

Module B3 — Living and Growing

Meiosis, Gametes and Fertilisation

Q1   Choose from the following words to complete the passage below.

haploid	meiosis	sperm	two copies	mitosis
cytoplasm	one copy	diploid	egg	

Gametes are the .... and .... cells. They're formed by a

process called .... In mammals, all body cells are ....,

which means they contain .... of each chromosome. However, gametes

are ...., which means they contain .... of each chromosome.

Q2   Tick the boxes to show whether the following statements are **true** or **false**.

The name is Goat. Zy Goat.

		True	False
a)	Fertilisation reduces genetic variation.	☐	☐
b)	At fertilisation gametes combine to form a haploid zygote.	☐	☐
c)	Genes on the chromosomes combine to control the characteristics of the zygote.	☐	☐

Q3 a)   Describe what happens in:

   i) The **first** meiotic division.

   ....

   ii) The **second** meiotic division.

   ....

b)   Explain how this produces cells that are genetically different.

   ....

   ....

Q4   **Sperm** are adapted to fertilising egg cells. Suggest how the
following features make sperm cells adapted to their function:

a)   many mitochondria.

   ....

b)   an acrosome.

   ....

Stem Cells, Differentiation and Growth

Q1 Tick the box next to the correct definition of **stem cells**.

1. Cells found only in embryos. ☐

2. Cells in plants that form the tissues within stems. ☐

3. Undifferentiated cells that can develop into different types of cells, tissues and organs. ☐

4. Undifferentiated cells that develop into a particular type of cell, tissue or organ. ☐

Q2 Give three differences in the **growth** of plants and animals.

1. ....

2. ....

3. ....

Q3 In the future, **embryonic stem cells** might be used to replace faulty cells in sick people.

a) How are **embryonic** stem cells different from **adult** stem cells?

....

....

b) Suggest one way in which embryonic stem cells could be used to treat a medical condition.

....

....

Q4 People have **different opinions** when it comes to **stem cell research**.

a) Give one argument **in favour** of stem cell research.

....

....

b) Give one argument **against** stem cell research.

....

....

Growth

Q1 Keeley wants to measure the growth of her pet batpig.

   a) Suggest one **advantage** of measuring the batpig's growth using:

     i) length ....

     ii) wet mass ....

     iii) dry mass ....

   b) Suggest one **disadvantage** of measuring the batpig's growth using only:

     i) length ....

     ii) wet mass ....

     iii) dry mass ....

   c) Which of the methods above is the best way of measuring growth?

    ....

Q2 The graph on the right is an example of a **human growth curve**.
It shows three different phases of growth.

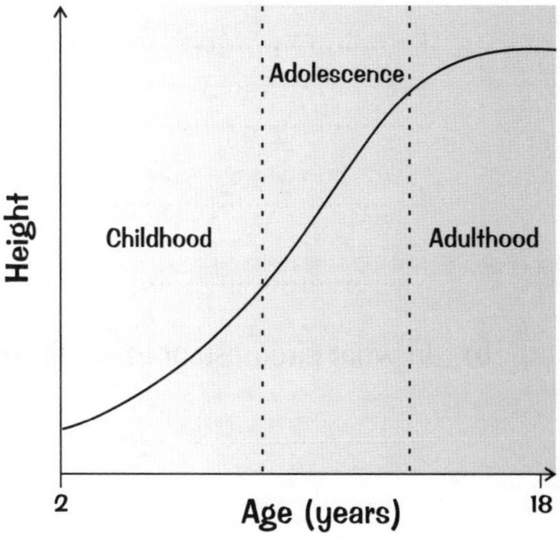

   a) Describe the trend in growth shown during **childhood**.

    ....

    ....

   b) **i)** During which phase on this growth curve
is growth **fastest**?

    ....

    ii) Name another phase of **rapid human growth**,
which is not shown on this growth curve.

    ....

Q3 Different parts of an organism grow at **different rates**.
Give one example of this and explain the reason behind it.

....

....

....

Respiration

Q1   **Respiration** happens in every cell in your body.

a) Complete the **chemical equation** below for **aerobic respiration**:

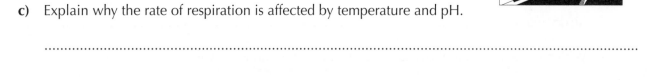

.... + ... $6O_2$ → $6CO_2$ .... + ... (+ ....)

b) Circle the correct word in each pair below to complete the sentences.

i) The energy released by respiration is used to
break down / **make** a small molecule called **ATM** / **ATP**.

ii) This molecule is the source of **oxygen** / **energy**
for lots of cell reactions.

c) Explain why the rate of respiration is affected by temperature and pH.

....

....

Q2   Humans can respire **aerobically** or **anaerobically**.

a) Give two disadvantages of **anaerobic** respiration compared to aerobic respiration.

1. ....

....

2. ....

....

b) In what circumstances would someone use anaerobic respiration?

....

....

c) Write the **word equation** for anaerobic respiration in humans.

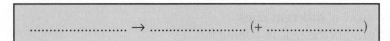

.... → .... (+ ....)

Top Tips: If you want to nail the respiration questions in the exam, make sure you know the
difference between aerobic and anaerobic respiration — aerobic is with oxygen, anaerobic is without.
And it's the presence or absence of oxygen that causes different products to be made.

Respiration

Q3   Judy decided to measure the **respiratory quotient** of two mice.
Her data is presented in the table below.

	Oxygen Used (cm³)	Carbon Dioxide Produced (cm³)
Mouse A	26.5	31.8
Mouse B	29.1	26.2

$$RQ = \frac{\text{Amount of } CO_2 \text{ produced}}{\text{Amount of } O_2 \text{ used}}$$

Calculate the respiratory quotient of each mouse using the formula given above.

a) Mouse A: ....

b) Mouse B: ....

Q4   Jim takes part in a race. The **graph** below shows Jim's
oxygen consumption before, during and after the race.

a) **i)** Describe what happens to Jim's oxygen
consumption **during** and **after** the race.

....

....

....

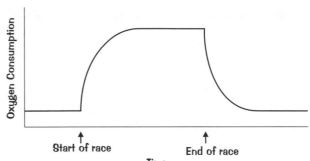

ii) What does this show about his respiration rate?

....

iii) What can Jim's rate of oxygen consumption be used to estimate?

....

b) Jim's leg muscles are painful after the race. Suggest what substance caused the pain.

....

c) Why does Jim's **breathing rate** not return to normal immediately after the race?

....

....

d) Why does Jim's **heart rate** not return to normal immediately after the race?

....

....

Functions of the Blood

Q1 **Plasma** carries just about everything around the body.

a) What is plasma?

....

b) Which of the following is a **digested food product** carried by plasma?
Circle the correct answer.

starch   protein   glucose   oxygen

c) i) Suggest one **waste product** carried by plasma.

....

ii) Where is this waste product carried from and to?

....

d) Name three other things carried by plasma.

1. ....

2. ....

3. ....

Q2 Use the words below to complete the passage about the structure of **red blood cells**.

Some words can be used more than once.

body tissues	large	biconcave	small	nucleus
carbon dioxide	oxygen	capillaries	haemoglobin	oxyhaemoglobin

Red blood cells are .... in shape, which means they have

a .... surface area to volume ratio for absorbing oxygen.

They have no ...., but their cytoplasm is full of

...................................., which combines with ....

in the lungs to form .... In ....,

the reverse of this reaction happens to release .... to

the cells. Red blood cells are very flexible, which means that they can fit

easily through the ....

Blood Vessels

Q1 Draw lines to match each of the words below with its correct description.

vein	vessel involved in the exchange of materials at the tissues
valve	vessel that takes blood away from the heart
artery	keeps the blood flowing in the right direction
lumen	vessel that takes blood to the heart
capillary	hole in the middle of a tube

HMS DRACULA

Q2 Circle the correct word in each of the sentences below.

a) **Arteries / Veins** contain valves to prevent the blood going backwards.

b) **Capillaries / Veins** have walls that are permeable.

c) **Veins / Arteries** have walls that are thick and muscular.

d) The blood pressure in the **arteries / veins** is higher than in the **arteries / veins**.

Q3 Two blood vessels are dissected from a piece of meat. One is a **vein** and the other is an **artery**. Measurements taken from both vessels are shown in the table below.

	Thickness of wall (mm)	Diameter of lumen (mm)
Blood vessel A	1.2	3.9
Blood vessel B	0.5	5.2

a) i) Which blood vessel would you expect to be the **vein**? Explain your answer.

....

....

ii) Suggest one way you could confirm this.

....

b) When tested, one of the blood vessels was found to be much more **elastic** than the other. Which one would you expect this to be? Explain your answer.

....

....

The Heart

Q1   The diagram below shows the human **heart**, as seen from the front.
The left atrium has been labelled. Complete the remaining labels **a)** to **j).**

a) ....

b) ....

c) ....

d) ....

e) ....

f) ....

g) ....

left atrium

h) ....

i) ....

j) ....

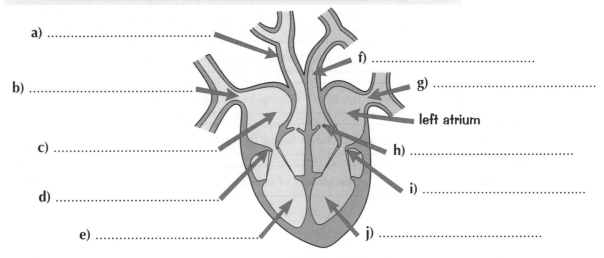

Q2   Mammals have a **double circulatory system** in which blood is pumped by the heart.

a)   What is a double circulatory system?

....

b)   Explain why having a double circulatory system is an advantage for mammals

....

....

....

Q3   Valves are present in the left and right ventricles of the heart.

a)   What is the function of the heart valves?

....

b)   Describe the function of the ventricles.

....

c)   Explain why the wall of the left ventricle is thicker than the wall of the right ventricle.

....

....

Top Tips: When doctors use a stethoscope to listen to your heart, it's actually the valves
closing that they hear. Make sure you understand why there are valves in the heart and veins.

Selective Breeding

Q1 Garfield wants to selectively breed one type of plant for its **fruit**, and another as an **ornamental house plant**.

a) What is selective breeding?

....

....

b) Suggest **two** characteristics that Garfield could select for in each kind of plant.

Fruit plant: ....

Ornamental house plant: ....

Q2 Describe two long term **disadvantages** of selective breeding.

1. ....

....

2. ....

....

Q3 Many breeds of **domesticated dog** have been bred for their **friendly temperament**.

a) Describe how selective breeding from an **aggressive** wolf-like stock of dogs could produce a breed with a more **friendly** temperament.

....

....

....

b) Explain why some domesticated dog breeds are likely to suffer from genetic disorders.

....

....

....

Genetic Engineering

Q1 **Genetic engineering** has produced a range of useful products.

a) Put the following stages of genetic engineering in order by numbering them 1–4.

☐ The gene is inserted into the DNA of another organism.

☐ The gene is cut from the DNA and isolated.

☐ The organism replicates.

☐ The gene for the characteristic is selected.

b) i) Suggest one **advantage** of genetic engineering.

....

ii) Suggest one **risk** of genetic engineering.

....

c) Describe one example of genetic engineering involving bacteria.

....

Q2 Plants can be genetically engineered.

a) Describe how genetic engineering can be used in **rice** to prevent Vitamin A deficiency.

....

....

b) Suggest how genetic engineering could improve crop yield.

....

Q3 Some people are **worried** about the ethical issues involved in genetic engineering.

a) Explain why this is.

....

....

b) Do you think that scientists should be carrying out genetic engineering? Explain your answer.

....

....

Gene Therapy and Cloning Animals

Q1 **Dolly** the sheep was cloned from an adult cell.

a) What are clones?

....

b) Name the **method** of cloning used to produce Dolly.

....

c) Write the correct letter (A, B, C or D) in the box next to each stage below to show where it belongs on the diagram.

A nucleus is removed from a sheep's egg cell. ☐

The embryo is implanted in the uterus of a surrogate mother sheep. ☐

A nucleus from an udder cell of a different sheep is inserted into the egg cell. ☐

The egg cell is given an electric shock to make it start dividing. ☐

Q2 In the future it might be possible to treat some health disorders using **gene therapy**.

a) What is gene therapy?

....

....

b) Tick the box next to the statement which is **true**.

Gene therapy can only be used to alter the genes of body cells. ☐

Gene therapy can only be used to alter the genes of gametes. ☐

Gene therapy can be used to alter the genes of gametes or body cells. ☐

c) Explain why gene therapy involving gametes is controversial.

....

....

Uses and Risks of Cloning Animals

Q1 Some **animals** could be genetically engineered to have **organs** suitable for transplantation into humans.

a) Describe the possible use of **cloning** in producing these organs.

....

....

b) Describe **two risks** involved with cloning animals.

....

....

c) Describe another possible use of cloning animals.

....

....

Q2 Cloning could be used to produce **human** embryos.
Suggest **one** use for these embryos.

....

....

Q3 Summarise the **ethical** issues involved in cloning humans.

....

....

....

....

Top Tips: Hmmm, cloning. It's always in the news, with various mad scientists regularly claiming to have produced the first human clone. You have to take this type of story with a pinch of salt though, because the media often aren't too keen on letting the facts get in the way of a good story.

Module B3 — Living and Growing

Cloning Plants

Q1   Plants are often grown commercially using **tissue culture**.

a)   Number the boxes below to put the stages of tissue culture in the correct order.

☐   The tissue is grown in a growth medium under aseptic conditions.

☐   Several small pieces of tissue are removed from the parent plant.

☐   When the tissues produce shoots and roots they're moved to potting compost to carry on growing.

☐   A plant with the desired characteristics is chosen.

growth medium

b)   Suggest two substances that are needed in the growth medium.

1. ....   2. ....

c)   Why is the tissue grown under aseptic conditions?

....

Q2   Explain why cloning plant cells is easier than cloning animal cells.

....

....

Q3   Alfie is setting up a banana farm and is trying to decide whether or not to use **cloned** plants.

a)   Suggest two **advantages** of using cloned plants.

1. ....

....

2. ....

....

b)   Suggest two **disadvantages** of using cloned plants.

1. ....

2. ....

Mixed Questions — Module B3

Q1   Humans can respire **aerobically** and **anaerobically**.

a)   Give a definition of respiration, including where it happens in the body.

....

b)   Circle the correct word in each pair to complete the following sentences
about **anaerobic respiration** in humans.

i)   Anaerobic respiration is respiration without **glucose** / **oxygen**.

ii) The incomplete breakdown of glucose during anaerobic
respiration produces **lactic acid** / **water**.

iii) **Less** / **More** energy is released per glucose molecule during
anaerobic respiration than during aerobic respiration.

*I told you respiration
released energy.*

*Do you think
anyone will
notice I blew up
the house?*

c)   Explain why anaerobic respiration leads to an **oxygen debt**.

....

....

Q2   **Plants** and **animals** grow in different ways.

a)   Describe how plant growth differs from animal growth regarding:

i) cell enlargement

....

....

ii) cell division

....

....

iii) cell differentiation

....

....

b)   The growth of both plants and animals can be measured by recording how their **wet mass**
increases over time. Give one **disadvantage** of this.

....

Mixed Questions — Module B3

Q3 **a)** What unique characteristic do **embryonic stem cells** have which adult stem cells don't have?

....

b) Scientists have experimented with growing stem cells in different conditions.
What is the name of the process by which stem cells **divide** for growth?

....

c) Suggest why scientists are especially interested in **embryonic** stem cells.

....

....

d) Some people disagree with stem cell research on ethical grounds.
Describe one **ethical issue** surrounding stem cell research.

....

....

Q4 The diagram shows part of the **circulatory system**.

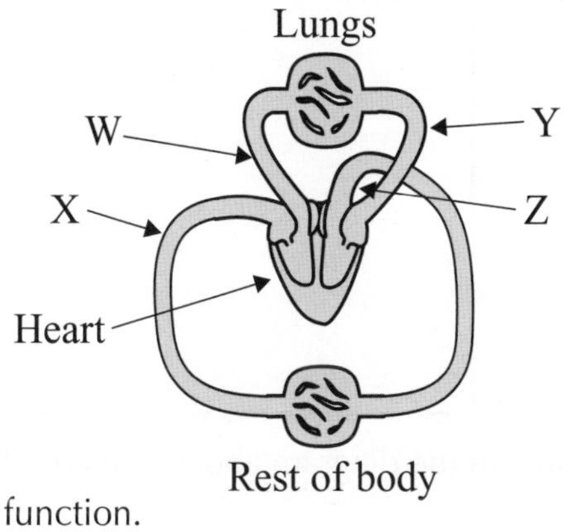

a) Name the blood vessels labelled W, X, Y and Z.

W ....

X ....

Y ....

Z ....

b) **i)** Explain how the structure of an artery is adapted for its function.

....

ii) Explain how the structure of a capillary is adapted for its function.

....

c) **i)** Which type of blood vessel contains valves?

....

ii) What is the function of these valves?

....

Module B3 — Living and Growing

Mixed Questions — Module B3

Q5 The sequence of bases in part of one strand of a **DNA** molecule is as follows:

A–A–T–C–C–A–A–T–C

a) Write down the **complementary sequence** of bases on the other strand of DNA.

....

b) Describe the relationship between DNA and proteins.

....

....

Q6 "Dolly the sheep" was produced in 1997 in Edinburgh, and was the world's first clone of an adult mammal. The diagram illustrates the process by which clones like Dolly can be produced.

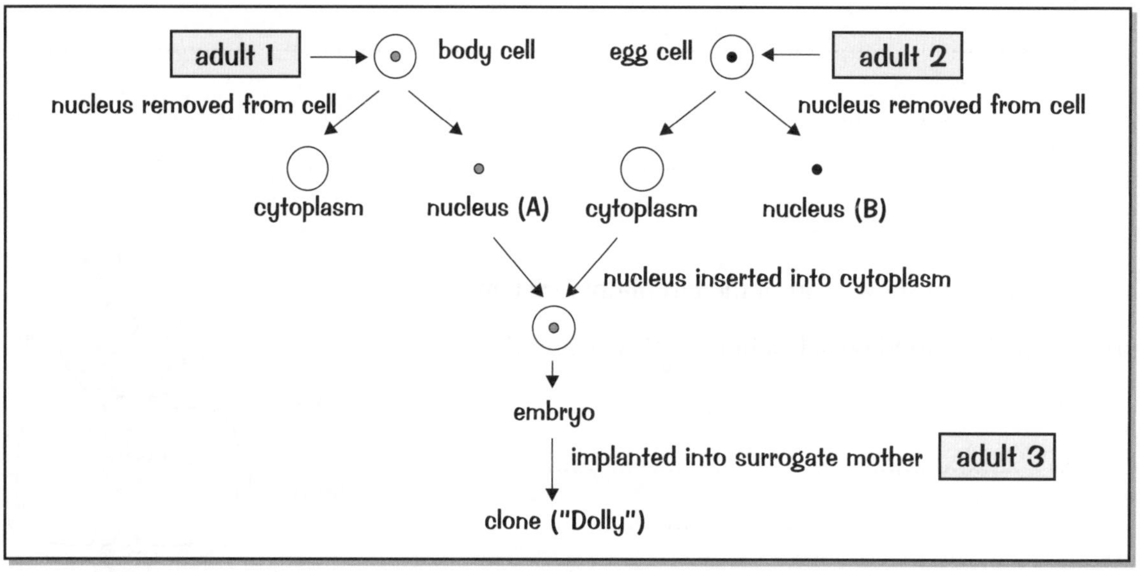

a) In the diagram above, which adult (1, 2 or 3) will the clone be identical to, and why?

....

....

b) An unfertilised sheep's egg contains 27 chromosomes. How many chromosomes will there be in:

i) the nucleus labelled A: ....

ii) the nucleus labelled B: ....

iii) the cloned sheep's body cells: ....

c) Suggest a potential benefit of cloning animals.

....

....

Atoms, Molecules and Compounds

Q1   Say whether each of the following refers to the **nucleus** or the **electrons** within an atom.

a) Has a negative charge. ....   **b)** Found at the centre of an atom. ....

c) Has a positive charge. ....   **d)** Involved in chemical bonding. ....

Q2   Circle the correct words from each pair to complete the sentences below.

a) If an atom **gains** / **loses** electrons it becomes a positive ion.

b) If an atom **gains** / **loses** electrons it becomes a negative ion.

c) When a negative ion is attracted to a positive ion they form **a covalent** / **an ionic** bond.

Q3   The diagram on the right shows a molecule of **butane**.

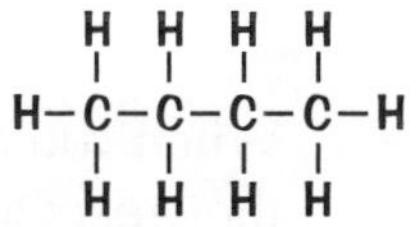

$$H-C-C-C-C-H$$ (with H atoms above and below each C)

Fill in the gaps in the following paragraph using words from the list below.

transferred	two	covalent	three	ionic	shared	charged	four

Butane is a compound containing .... different sorts of atoms.

The atoms join together because electrons are .... between them,

forming .... bonds.

Q4   The **molecular formula** of **octane** is $CH_3(CH_2)_6CH_3$.

a) How many atoms are there altogether in a molecule of octane? ....

b) How many carbon atoms are there in an octane molecule? ....

c) How many hydrogen atoms are there in an octane molecule? ....

Q5   Write out the **chemical formulas** of the following compounds.

a) carbon dioxide ....   **b)** calcium carbonate   ....   **c)** hydrochloric acid ....

d) water   ....   **e)** magnesium chloride ....   **f)** calcium chloride   ....

Q6   Complete the table showing the **names**, **displayed formulas**, **molecular formulas** and the number of **covalent bonds** for the carbon compounds.

NAME	DISPLAYED FORMULA	MOLECULAR FORMULA	NUMBER OF COVALENT BONDS
ETHANE	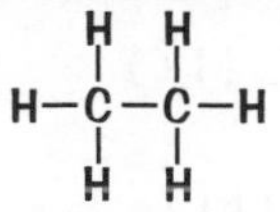 H-C-C-H (with H above and below each C)	**a)**	**b)**
PROPANE	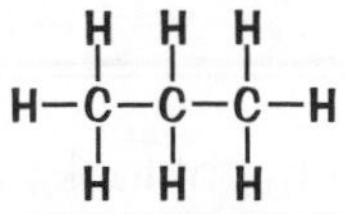 H-C-C-C-H (with H above and below each C)	**c)**	**d)**

Chemical Equations

Q1 Which of the following equations are **balanced** correctly? Tick the correct boxes.

Correctly balanced Incorrectly balanced

a) $H_2 + Cl_2 \rightarrow 2HCl$ ☐ ☐

b) $CuO + HCl \rightarrow CuCl_2 + H_2O$ ☐ ☐

c) $N_2 + H_2 \rightarrow NH_3$ ☐ ☐

d) $CuO + H_2 \rightarrow Cu + H_2O$ ☐ ☐

e) $CaCO_3 \rightarrow CaO + CO_2$ ☐ ☐

Q2 When you drop a strip of **magnesium** metal (Mg) into **sulfuric acid** (H_2SO_4), they react to give **magnesium sulfate** and **H_2 gas**.

a) Write the **word equation** for this reaction.

....

b) Write the **balanced symbol equation** for the reaction.

....

c) Explain how you can tell that the equation you wrote in part **b)** is **properly balanced**.

....

Q3 **Balance** these equations.

If a molecule doesn't need a number in front, just leave it blank — I've left spaces in front of them all so I don't give the game away.

a) .... K_2O + ... H_2O → .... KOH

b) .... $H-\overset{\displaystyle H}{\underset{\displaystyle H}{C}}-H$ + ... O=O → .... O=C=O + ... $H\diagup^{O}\diagdown H$

c) .... Br_2 + ... Al → .... $AlBr_3$

d) .... $H-\overset{\displaystyle H}{\underset{\displaystyle H}{C}}-\overset{\displaystyle OH}{\underset{\displaystyle H}{C}}-H$ + ... O=O → .... O=C=O + ... $H\diagup^{O}\diagdown H$

e) .... $CaCO_3$ + ... HCl → .... $CaCl_2$ + ... CO_2 + ... H_2O

f) .... $Mg(OH)_2$ + ... H_2SO_4 → .... $MgSO_4$ + ... H_2O

g) .... Fe_2O_3 + ... H_2SO_4 → .... $Fe_2(SO_4)_3$ + ... H_2O

Top Tips: Balancing equations isn't quite as scary as it might look. All you have to do is juggle the numbers in front of the chemicals till you've got the same number of each type of atom on both sides.

Energy Transfer in Reactions

Q1 Use the words to **complete** the passage below. Each word can be used more than once.

| endothermic | exothermic | energy | heat | an increase | a decrease |

All chemical reactions involve changes in ....

In .... reactions, ... energy is given out to the

surroundings. A thermometer will show .... in temperature.

In .... reactions, ... energy is taken in from the

surroundings. A thermometer will show .... in temperature.

Q2 Fiz investigated the **temperature change** during a reaction.
She added 25 cm³ of sodium hydroxide solution to 25 cm³
of hydrochloric acid. She recorded the temperature of the
reaction mixture at **15 second intervals** for **two minutes**.

Fiz plotted her results on the graph shown.

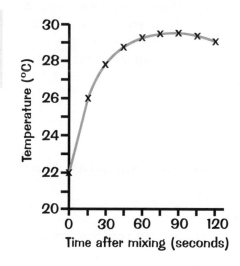

a) What was the increase in temperature due to the reaction?

....

b) Circle any of the words below that correctly describe
the reaction in this experiment.

decomposition   combustion
endothermic   respiration   exothermic

Q3 **Circle** the correct words to complete each of the sentences below.

a) An example of an endothermic reaction is **thermal decomposition / combustion**.

b) Bond breaking is an **exothermic / endothermic** process.

c) Bond making is an **exothermic / endothermic** process.

Q4 As the reaction shown below takes place, the temperature of the reaction mixture **increases**.

A B + C ⟶ A C + B

a) Is this reaction exothermic or endothermic? ....

b) Which bond is stronger, A–B or A–C? Explain your answer.

....

....

Measuring the Energy Content of Fuels

Q1   Write down the formulas for calculating:

a)   the energy transferred to water during a calorimetric experiment.

....

b)   the energy output of a fuel per gram.

....

Q2   Ross wants to compare the **energy content** of two fuels, petrol and a petrol alternative, fuel X.

a)   In the box on the right,
draw a labelled diagram
showing the apparatus
Ross could use to compare
the energy content of the
two fuels in a simple
calorimetric experiment.

b)   Name **two variables** that Ross has to **control** to ensure a fair test when using this method.

....

c)   Suggest how Ross could make sure that his results were **reliable**.

....

d)   He finds that **0.7 g** of petrol raises the temperature of **50 g** of water by **30.5 °C**.

i)   Calculate the energy gained by the water.

....

ii) Use your answer to **i)** to calculate the energy produced per gram of petrol.
Give your answer in units of **kJ/g**.

....

e)   Burning **0.8 g** of fuel X raises the temperature of **50 g** of water by **27 °C**.
Calculate the energy produced per gram of fuel X.

....

....

f)   Using this evidence only, decide whether petrol or fuel X would make the better fuel.
Explain your choice.

....

Chemical Reaction Rates

Q1   Match these common chemical reactions to the **speed** at which they happen.

a firework exploding	**SLOW (hours or longer)**	iron rusting
hair being dyed	**MODERATE SPEED (minutes)**	a match burning
an apple rotting	**FAST (seconds or shorter)**	oil paint drying

Q2   Tick the boxes to show whether the following statements are **true** or **false**.

                                                                                True False

a)   When particles collide they always react. ☐ ☐

b)   The greater the frequency of collisions, the greater the rate of reaction. ☐ ☐

c)   Collision theory helps us to explain rates of reaction. ☐ ☐

Q3   Two particles are moving around in a reaction mixture. Name **two** factors that determine whether or not they will **react** with each other.

1. ....

2. ....

Q4   Joe measured the **rate** of a reaction. He added 1 g of **calcium carbonate powder** to 100 cm³ of **dilute hydrochloric acid**. The equation for the reaction that took place is shown below.

$$CaCO_3 + 2HCl \rightarrow CaCl_2 + CO_2 + H_2O$$

Think about the states of the products.

a)   Joe measured the reaction rate by recording how the mass of the mixture changed over time. After two minutes there was still some powder left at the bottom of the flask, but the mass of the reaction mixture had stopped changing.

    i) State which reactant is the limiting reactant ....

    ii) Explain your answer to part **i)**. ....

    ....

b)   Joe is going to repeat the experiment. This time he plans to add half as much of the limiting reactant. What will happen to the amount of calcium chloride produced? Explain your answer.

....

....

....

Collision Theory

Q1 Draw lines to match up the changes with their effects on the particles.

increasing the temperature

decreasing the concentration

adding a catalyst

increasing the surface area

provides a surface for particles to stick to and lowers activation energy

makes the particles move faster, so they collide more often

means more of a solid reactant will be exposed to particles of the other reactant

means fewer particles of reactants are present, so fewer collisions occur

Q2 Reactions involving gases are affected by the **pressure**.

a) In the boxes on the right, draw two diagrams, one showing particles of two different gases at low pressure, the other showing the gases at high pressure.

b) i) If you increase the pressure of reacting gases, will the rate of reaction **increase** or **decrease**? ....

ii) Explain your answer.

....

....

low pressure   high pressure

Q3 Here are five statements about **surface area** and rates of reaction. Tick the appropriate box to show whether each is **true** or **false**.

True False

a) Breaking a solid into smaller pieces decreases its surface area.

b) A larger surface area will mean a faster rate of reaction.

c) A larger surface area decreases the number of useful collisions.

d) Powdered marble has a larger surface area than the same mass of marble chips.

e) A powdered solid reactant produces more product overall than an equal mass of reactant in large lumps does.

Q4 Circle the correct words to complete the sentences below.

a) In order for a reaction to occur, the particles must **remain still / collide**.

b) If you make a solution more concentrated it means there are **more / less** reactant particles in the same volume.

c) This means that the reactant particles are **more / less** likely to collide with each other.

d) So, increasing the concentration **increases / decreases** the rate of reaction.

Collision Theory

Q5 Choose words from the list below to complete the paragraph.

successful	slowing down	slower	speeding up
faster	energy	decreases	increases

When a reacting mixture is heated, the particles move ....

This .... the frequency of collisions. It also gives the particles

more .... so more collisions are ....

All this leads to the reaction ....

Q6 The sign on the right is displayed on the doors of a factory that makes **custard powder**. Other than hygiene, explain why these rules are important.

DANGER
NO SMOKING,
MATCHES OR
OPEN LIGHTS

....

....

....

Q7 Karen's chemistry teacher gives her a sample of a mystery chemical.
He tells her that the chemical is a catalyst for this reaction: $2H_2O_2 \rightarrow O_2 + 2H_2O$

a) Explain what a catalyst is.

....

....

b) How much of the catalyst does Karen need to add in order to increase the reaction rate?
Circle the best answer below.

A very small amount.   **A very large amount.**

c) Karen tries adding a bit of the mystery chemical to a different reaction.
Is it likely that the mystery chemical will speed up this reaction too? Explain your answer.

....

....

Top Tips: Collision theory is all about the probability of reactants bumping into each other.
Anything that makes things bump more often will also increase the rate of the reaction.

Rate of Reaction Data

Q1 Sam conducted two experiments with equal masses of marble chips and equal volumes of hydrochloric acid (HCl). He used two **different concentrations** of acid and measured the **change in mass** of the reactants. Below is a graph of the results.

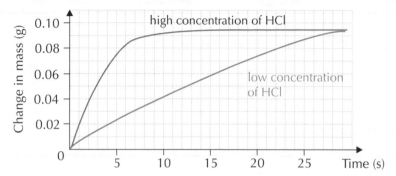

acid concentration

a) Calculate the average rate of reaction for the first five seconds for:

i) the experiment carried out with a high concentration of HCl.

....

ii) the experiment carried out with a low concentration of HCl.

....

b) Circle the letter(s) next to any valid conclusion(s) below that you might draw **from this graph**.

A   Increasing the concentration of the acid has no effect on the rate of reaction.

B   Rate of reaction depends on the acid concentration.

C   Rate of reaction depends on the mass of the marble chips.

c) State what the **change in mass** will be for the experiment with the high concentration of HCl after **35 seconds**.   ....

Q2 Eve investigated how **surface area** affects reaction rate. She added excess dilute hydrochloric acid to **large marble chips** and measured the loss of mass at regular intervals. She repeated the experiment using the same mass of **powdered marble**. Below is a graph of her results.

a) Which curve, A or B, was obtained when **large pieces** of marble were used? ....

b) On the graph opposite, draw:

i) the curve you would expect from the **same mass** of **medium** sized marble pieces. Label it C.

ii) the curve you would expect from **half** the mass of medium sized marble pieces. Label it D.

c) Is there enough information given above for you to be sure whether this was a **fair test** or not? Explain your answer.

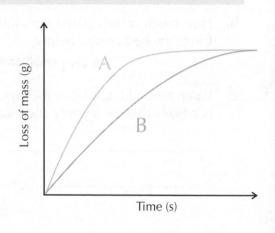

....

....

Rate of Reaction Data

Q3 Pete measured how much **carbon dioxide** was given off during the reaction between 5 g of **marble chips** (calcium carbonate) and 100 cm³ of **hydrochloric acid**. His data is shown below.

Time (s)	REACTION 1 Volume of CO_2 produced (cm³)	REACTION 2 Volume of CO_2 produced (cm³)
10	14	24
20	25	42
30	36	57
40	46	69
50	54	77
60	62	80
70	70	80
80	76	80
90	80	80
100	80	80

a) On the grid below, plot a graph of **volume of carbon dioxide** (vertical axis) against **time** (horizontal axis) for **reaction 1**. Label it.

b) On the same axes, plot a similar graph for **reaction 2**. Label it.

c) State which reaction is faster. Explain how you know this.

....

d) Suggest **three** things Pete might have done differently for **reaction 2** to cause the change in **rate**.

1. ....

2. ....

3. ....

e) On your graph label where: **i)** reaction 2 **finished**.
                                      ii) reaction 2 had its **fastest rate**.

f) Calculate the rate of reaction for both reaction 1 and reaction 2 for the first 20 s.

....

....

g) Does this back up your answer to part **c)**? ....

h) What volume of carbon dioxide had been produced in **reaction 1** after **25 seconds**? .... Read the value off the graph you have drawn.

Top Tips: So, that's it in a nutshell — the faster a reaction goes, the steeper its graph will be, and when the reaction stops, the graph levels out. It's as easy as falling off a chemistry-based log... Ouch...

Reacting Masses

34

Q1   What are the **relative atomic masses** (A_r) of the following:

   a) Magnesium ....

   b) Neon ....

   c) Oxygen ....

   d) Hydrogen ....

   e) C ....

   f) Cu ....

   g) K ....

   h) Ca ....

   i) Cl ....

Q2   Calculate the **relative formula masses** (M_r) of the following:

   a) Water, H_2O ....

   b) Nitric acid, HNO_3 ....

   c) Ammonium nitrate, NH_4NO_3 ....

   d) Calcium nitrate, $Ca(NO_3)_2$ ....

Q3   The balanced symbol equation below shows a reaction between **potassium** and **water**.

$$2K + 2H_2O \rightarrow 2KOH + H_2$$

   a) Use relative formula masses to show that **mass is conserved** during this reaction

   ....

   ....

   ....

   b) Explain why the **products** of a chemical reaction have **the same mass** as the **reactants**.

   ....

   ....

   ....

Q4   Tim heats 3.175 g of **copper** with **sulfur** to form **copper sulfide**.

   Calculate how much copper sulfide will be produced using the masses of copper shown in the table below. All the copper reacts with all the sulfur to form copper sulfide.

   Copper sulfide is the only product formed in this reaction.

Mass of copper / g	Mass of sulfur / g	Mass of copper sulfide / g
63.5	32	
31.75		
3.175		

Module C3 — Chemical Economics

Calculating Masses in Reactions

Q1 Anna burns **10 g** of **magnesium** in air to produce **magnesium oxide** (MgO).

a) Write out the **balanced equation** for this reaction.

....

b) Calculate the mass of **magnesium oxide** that's produced.

....

....

....

Q2 What mass of **sodium** (Na) is needed to make **2 g** of **sodium oxide** (Na$_2$O)?

> The equation for this reaction is
> $4Na + O_2 \rightarrow 2Na_2O$

....

....

....

Q3 **Aluminium** and **iron oxide** (Fe$_2$O$_3$) react together to produce **aluminium oxide** (Al$_2$O$_3$) and **iron**.

a) Write out the **balanced equation** for this reaction.

....

b) What **mass** of iron is produced from **20 g** of iron oxide?

....

....

....

Q4 **Propane** (C$_3$H$_8$) burns in **oxygen** (O$_2$) to give **carbon dioxide** (CO$_2$) and **water** (H$_2$O).

How many grams of propane would you need to burn to make **1.65 g** of **carbon dioxide**?

....

....

....

....

<u>*Atom Economy*</u>

Q1   **Copper oxide** can be reduced to copper by burning it with carbon.

> **copper ore + carbon → copper + carbon dioxide**
>
> **2CuO + C → 2Cu + CO$_2$**
>
> Relative formula masses: **CuO = 79.5, C = 12, Cu = 63.5, CO$_2$ = 44**

a)   What is the useful product in this reaction? ....

b)   Calculate the **atom economy** of the reaction. ....

....

c)   Calculate what percentage of the starting materials are wasted.

....

Q2   Explain why industrial reactions with a **high atom economy** are better than reactions with a **low atom economy**.

....

....

....

Q3   The two reactions shown below are both used industrially to make **ethanol** (CH$_3$CH$_2$OH).

     Reaction 1: **C$_2$H$_4$ + H$_2$O → CH$_3$CH$_2$OH**   **Reaction 2:** **C$_6$H$_{12}$O$_6$ → 2CH$_3$CH$_2$OH + 2CO$_2$**

a)   State which of these two reactions has a 100% atom economy. ....

b)   Give a reason for your answer to part **a)**.

....

....

Q4   **Titanium** can be reduced from titanium chloride (TiCl$_4$) using magnesium or sodium.

a)   Work out the atom economy for each reaction.

    With magnesium: TiCl$_4$ + 2Mg → Ti + 2MgCl$_2$ ....

....

    With sodium: TiCl$_4$ + 4Na → Ti + 4NaCl ....

....

b)   Which one has the better atom economy? ....

Percentage Yield

Q1 James wanted to produce **silver chloride** (AgCl). He added a carefully measured mass of silver nitrate to an excess of dilute hydrochloric acid. An **insoluble white salt** formed.

   a) Write down the formula for calculating the **percentage yield** of a reaction.

   b) James calculated that he should get 2.7 g of silver chloride, but he only got 1.2 g. What was the **percentage yield**?

....

....

Q2 The **percentage yield** of industrial processes needs to be as high as possible.

   a) Explain why chemical reactions that are used in industry need to have high percentage yields.

....

....

   b) Explain why **evaporation** can affect the percentage yield of a reaction.

....

....

....

Q3 Aaliya and Natasha mixed together barium chloride ($BaCl_2$) and sodium sulfate (Na_2SO_4) in a beaker. An **insoluble** substance formed. They **filtered** the solution to obtain the solid substance, and then transferred the solid to a clean piece of **filter paper** and left it to dry.

   a) Aaliya calculated that they should produce a yield of **15 g** of barium sulfate. However, after completing the experiment they found they had only obtained **6 g**.

Calculate the **percentage yield** for this reaction.

....

....

   b) Suggest two reasons why their actual yield was lower than their predicted yield.

1. ....

2. ....

Chemical Production

Q1   Suggest whether **continuous** or **batch** production would be used to make the following chemicals.

   a)   Perfumes   ....

   b)   Sulfuric acid   ....

   c)   Ammonia   ....

   d)   Paints   ....

Q2   Widely used chemicals are often produced by **continuous production**.

   a)   Circle the correct words to complete the following sentences.

   > Continuous production is often used for the **small-scale / large-scale** production of chemicals.
   >
   > It's **highly automated / labour-intensive**, which means that there are low labour costs.
   >
   > Continuous production means that the quality of products is very **consistent / inconsistent**.

   b)   State two **disadvantages** of continuous production.

   1. ....

   2. ....

Q3   **Batch production** is used to produce specialist chemicals.

   a)   Use these words to complete the blanks about batch production.

   inflexible   high   small   quality   large   versatile   low

   > Batch production is often used for manufacturing .... quantities
   >
   > of specialist chemicals. The advantages of batch production are that the plant is
   >
   > .... (allowing for many different products to be made), and that the
   >
   > costs of plant equipment are .... Disadvantages of batch production
   >
   > include the .... labour costs and the difficulties in maintaining the same
   >
   > .... of product from batch to batch.

   b)   Why are **pharmaceutical drugs** usually manufactured using batch production?

   ....

   ....

Chemical Production

Q4 Compounds used in pharmaceutical drugs are often extracted from **plants**.

a) Describe the following steps in the extraction process.

A   B   C

Step A ....

Step B ....

Step C ....

b) Give **two** reasons why companies spend money and time on trials for new drugs.

1. ....

2. ....

c) i) The melting temperature of a drug is 82 °C. State which of the following
samples is a pure sample of the drug and give a reason for your answer.

Sample 1 = 80 ° C   Sample 2 = 82 °C   Sample 3 = 86 °C

....

....

ii) Step C is carried out on a pure sample of the drug.
Describe and explain what the results of Step C would look like.

....

....

Q5 Tony decides his pharmaceutical company should develop and manufacture a new drug.

a) Give two reasons why the **research** and **development** of new pharmaceutical drugs is expensive.

1. ....

2. ....

b) Give two reasons why the **manufacturing** process of pharmaceutical drugs is expensive.

1. ....

2. ....

Allotropes of Carbon

Q1   Diamond, **graphite**, and **fullerenes** are all **allotropes** of carbon.

a) Explain the meaning of the term '**allotropes**'.

....

b) The structures of **three** allotropes of carbon are shown below.
Write the **name** of each allotrope under the diagrams.

i)

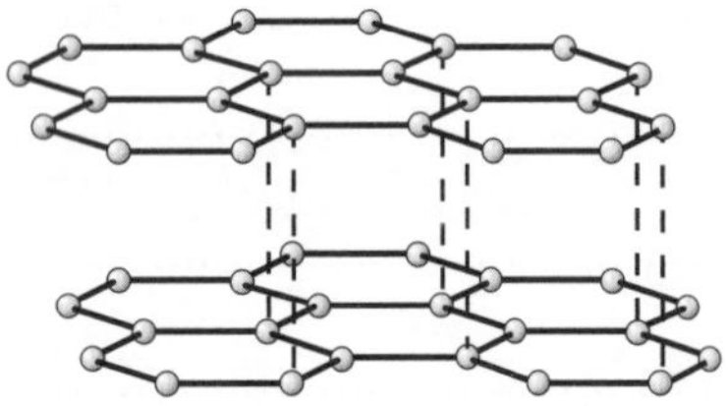

....

ii)

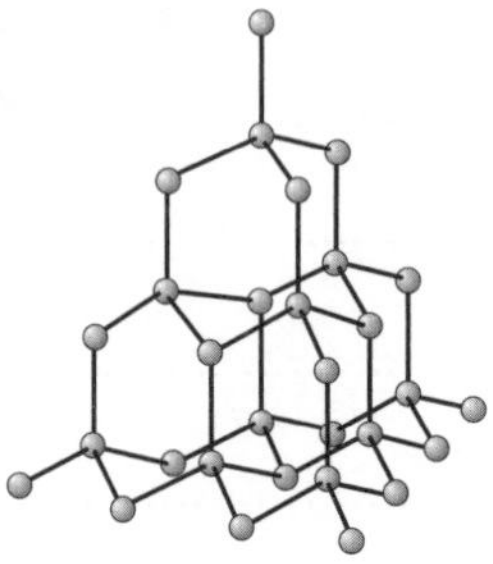

....

iii)

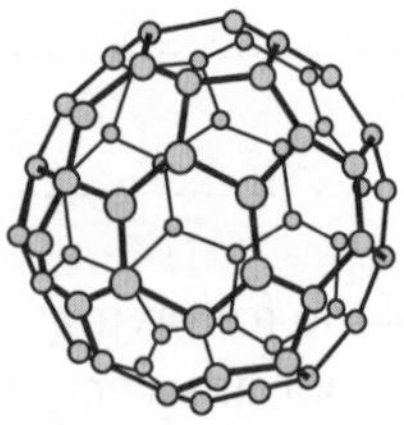

....

c) Both diamond and graphite are giant molecular structures.
Give **two** properties of a giant molecular structure.

1. ....

2. ....

Q2   **Fullerenes** are an allotrope of carbon.

a) Fullerenes can be used to 'cage' other molecules. Give a potential use for this technology.

....

b) What are **nanotubes**?

....

c) Briefly explain why nanotubes are used to make **industrial catalysts**.

....

....

Top Tips: There's more than one allotrope of carbon you've got to know about and you need
to know what they are, what their uses are and why they're suitable for these uses. Hmmm, thrilling.

Allotropes of Carbon

Q3 **Graphite** is an allotrope of carbon.

a) Fill in the gaps in the passage using words from the list below.

four	red	tools	lubricant	tightly	three	high
low	black	loosely	slide	delocalised		

Graphite is made of layers of carbon that are held .... together.

It is .... in colour. Within the layers, each carbon atom forms

.... covalent bonds. These strong covalent bonds give graphite a

.... melting point. Between the layers there is only a weak attraction.

This enables the layers to .... easily over each other, which makes it

useful as a ....

b) Explain why graphite is **able** to conduct electricity.

....

....

c) Give two reasons why graphite is used in pencil leads.

1. ....

2. ....

Q4 **Diamond** is another allotrope of carbon.

a) Circle the correct words to complete the sentences below about diamond.

Diamond has a **simple molecular / giant covalent** structure. Each carbon atom in
diamond forms **three / four** covalent bonds with neighbouring atoms.
Because it has lots of strong covalent bonds diamond has a **low / high** melting point
and is very **soft / hard**, which makes it ideal for use in **lubricants / cutting tools**.

b) Why is diamond **unable** to conduct electricity?

....

c) Name two properties of diamond that make it useful for **jewellery**.

1. ....

2. ....

Mixed Questions — Module C3

Q1 Lee is investigating how changing the **concentration** of acid that he uses affects the rate of a reaction.

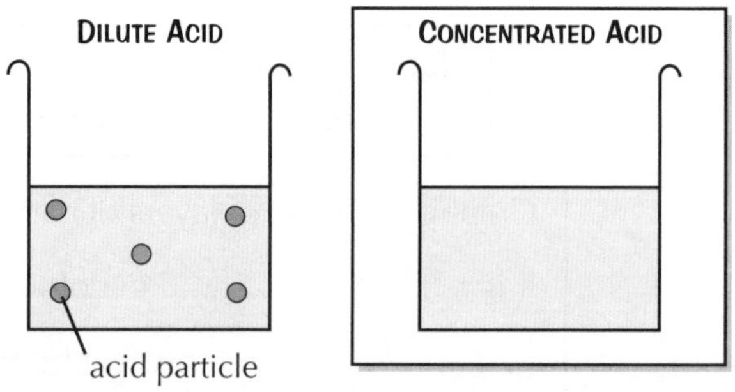

a) The diagram on the right shows the acid particles present in a solution of **dilute acid**.

In the box, complete the diagram showing the **same volume** of concentrated acid.

DILUTE ACID   CONCENTRATED ACID

acid particle

b) Explain how increasing the **concentration** of the acid will affect the reaction rate.

....

....

....

c) Using the axes on the right:

i) Sketch the reaction rate curve you would expect to see when Lee uses a **high** concentration of acid.

ii) Sketch the reaction rate curve you would expect to see when Lee uses a **low** concentration of acid.

(Assume that the acid is not the limiting reactant.)

d) Name two things Lee will need to keep constant in order to make it a **fair experiment**.

1. ....

2. ....

Q2 **30 g** of a fuel, X, is burnt and used to heat **100 g** of water. The temperature of the water before heating was **20 °C**, and after heating it was **42 °C**.

The specific heat capacity of water = 4.2 J/g °C

a) Calculate the energy transferred **per gram** of this fuel.

....

....

....

b) What name is given to a reaction like this one that gives out energy? ....

c) Which quantity of energy is the larger in this reaction? Underline the correct answer.

The energy required to break the old bonds.   The energy released in forming the new bonds.

Module C3 — Chemical Economics

Mixed Questions — Module C3

Q3 The graph on the right shows the results of three **rate of reaction experiments** using **magnesium** and dilute **hydrochloric acid**.

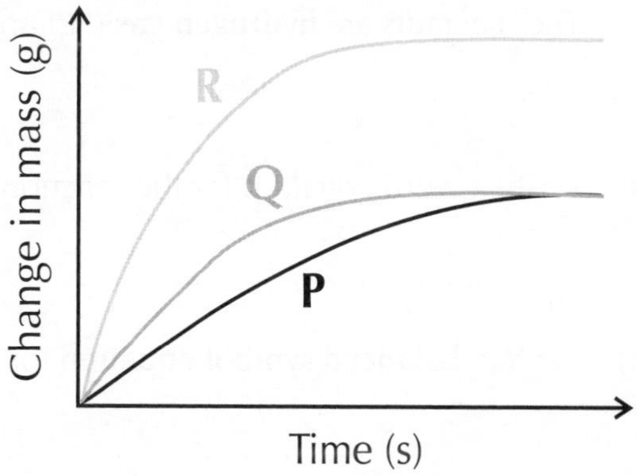

a) Which reaction was **faster**, P or Q?

....

b) Which reaction started off with the **largest** amount of limiting reactant, P, Q or R?

....

c) Mark with an X on the graph the point at which reaction R finished.

Q4 **Calcium carbonate** will thermally decompose to give **calcium oxide** and **carbon dioxide**.

a) Complete the **balanced symbol equation** for this reaction, shown below.

.... (s) → CaO (s) + ... (g)

b) Calculate the relative formula masses of:

i) Calcium carbonate ....

ii) Calcium oxide ....

iii) Carbon dioxide ....

c) This reaction is used industrially to produce **calcium oxide**.

i) Calculate the mass of calcium carbonate you would need to make **15 g** of calcium oxide.

....

....

....

ii) Calculate the **atom economy** of the reaction.

....

....

d) The thermal decomposition of calcium carbonate is **endothermic**. What will happen to the temperature of the surroundings as the reaction happens? Explain your answer.

....

....

Mixed Questions — Module C3

Q5 The **Haber Process** is used to manufacture **ammonia** (NH_3).
The reactants are **hydrogen gas** (H_2) and **nitrogen gas** (N_2).

a) Write a word equation for the reaction that creates ammonia.

....

b) Write a **balanced symbol equation** for the same reaction.

....

c) Calculate how much ammonia you would expect to produce
from 12 g of nitrogen gas.

> Nitrogen has an A_r of 14.
> Hydrogen has an A_r of 1.

....

....

....

....

d) The actual yield from 12 g of nitrogen gas is about 1.82 g of ammonia.
Calculate the percentage yield of the reaction.

> The yield of this reaction is
> low because it is **reversible**.
> To reduce waste, any unused
> reactants are **recycled**.

....

....

....

e) A solid iron catalyst is added to the reaction mixture.
Circle the correct words to complete the following sentences about the catalyst.

i) Adding an iron catalyst **increases / doesn't affect** the rate of the reaction
between nitrogen and hydrogen.

ii) Adding an iron catalyst **increases / doesn't affect** the yield of ammonia.

f) Ammonia is usually produced using **continuous production**.

i) Give one advantage of producing ammonia in this way.

....

ii) Give one disadvantage of producing ammonia in this way.

....

Speed and Distance

Q1 Ealing is about **12 km** west of Marble Arch. It takes a tube train **20 minutes** to get to Marble Arch from Ealing.

Circle the letter next to the true statement below.

A   The average speed of the train is 60 m/s.

B   The average speed of the train is 10 m/s.

C   The average speed of the train is 60 m/s due east.

D   The average speed of the train is 36 m/s.

	Albert Square		Marble Arch
Ealing		Walford East	

Q2 A pulse of laser light takes **1.3 seconds** to travel from the Moon to the Earth.

The speed of light is 3×10^8 **m/s**. How far away is the Moon from the Earth in **km**?

....

Q3 I rode my bike **1500 m** to the shops. It took me **5 minutes**.

a)   What was my **average speed** in m/s?

....

b)   Going home I took a different route and my average speed was **4 m/s**. It took me **8 minutes**. How far is the journey home?

....

c)   One part of the journey was downhill. I was travelling at **4 m/s** at the top of the hill and **11 m/s** at the bottom. It took **48 s** to get from the top of the hill to the bottom. What distance did I cover on this part of the journey?

....

d)   At the end of the journey I hit the brakes, slowed down at a constant rate and travelled **9 m** in **3 s** until I stopped. How fast was I travelling **when I started to brake**?

....

Q4 The **speed limit** for cars on the motorway is **70 mph** (about 31 m/s). A motorist accelerated onto the motorway from a service station and was captured on a speed camera. He denied speeding.

Look at his **distance-time** graph.
Was the motorist telling the truth?

....

....

....

....

Speed and Distance

Q5 Steve walked to football training only to find that he'd left his boots at home.
He turned round and walked back home, where he spent **30 seconds** looking for them.
To make it to training on time he had to run back at **twice** his walking speed.

Below is an **incomplete** distance-time graph for his journey.

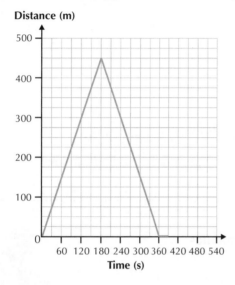

a) How long did it take Steve to **walk** to training?

....

b) Calculate Steve's speed for the
first section of the graph in m/s.

....

c) Complete the graph to show Steve's **run** back.

Remember, the gradient of a distance-time graph = speed.

Q6 The graph shows the motion of a **train** as it travels from Alphaville
to Charlietown, where it **stops** briefly, and then moves off again.

a) Describe the **motion** of the train in the sections marked:

A ....

B ....

C ....

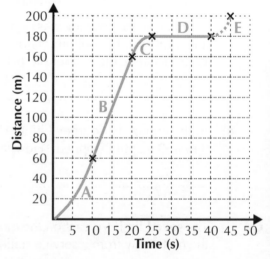

b) What is the train's **average** speed between
Alphaville and Charlietown?

....

....

c) Calculate the **maximum** speed of the train between the two stations.

....

....

d) How long does the train **stop** at Charlietown?

....

<u>*Speed and Acceleration*</u>

Q1 The monorail at Buffers' Theme Park takes people from the visitor centre to the main park and back again. It travels at the **same speed** on the outward and return journeys.

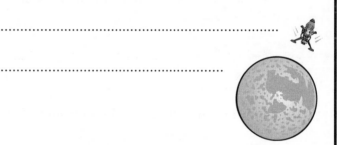

Buffers' Theme Park
| Monorail | Visitor |
| Main park | River | centre Car park |

The monorail's **velocity** on the outward journey is **12 m/s**. What is its velocity on the return journey?

....

Q2 Below is a speed-time graph for the descent of a lunar lander. It accelerates due to the pull of **gravity** from the Moon.

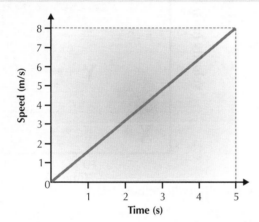

Use the graph to calculate this acceleration.

....

....

....

Q3 The Go Go car company make gas-powered model cars. One car **accelerates** from rest to **20 m/s** in **3.5 s**.

a) What is its **acceleration**?

....

b) The car is modified and now accelerates from 3 m/s to 20 m/s in 2.8 s. Suggest whether this modification has **improved** the car's acceleration. Show your working.

....

....

Q4 An egg is **dropped** from the top of the Eiffel tower. It hits the ground after **8 seconds**, at a speed of **80 m/s**.

a) Find the egg's acceleration.

....

b) How long did it take for the egg to reach **40 m/s**?

....

Speed and Acceleration

Q5   A car accelerates at **2 m/s²**. After 4 seconds it reaches a speed of **24 m/s**.

How fast was it going **before** it started to accelerate?

....

....

Q6   The graph on the right shows a speed-skater's performance during a race.

a)   How **far** does the skater go in the following sections:

X   ....

....

Y   ....

....

Z   ....

....

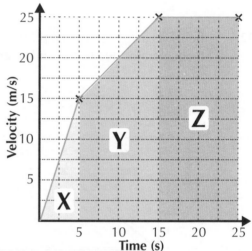

b)   If the race finishes after **25 s**, how far will she have travelled altogether?

....

Q7   Match each line on the **distance-time** graph with the correct line on the **velocity-time** graph.

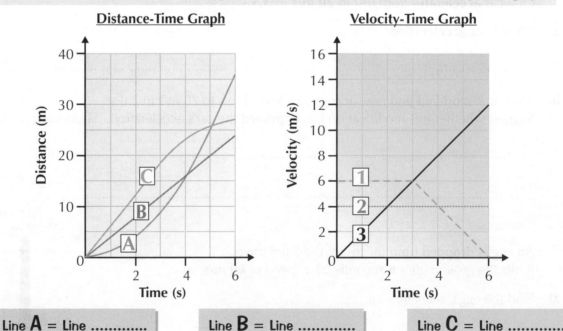

Line **A** = Line ....   Line **B** = Line ....   Line **C** = Line ....

Top Tips: The most confusing thing about Acceleration can be interpreting the graphs.
The key thing to remember on a V-T graph is that the steepness of the line is the acceleration.
If the line is curved, the acceleration is changing — the steeper the line, the greater the acceleration.

Module P3 — Forces for Transport

Mass, Weight and Gravity

Q1   Tick the boxes to show whether the following statements are **true** or **false**.

		True	False
a)	Gravity is affected by changes in the atmosphere.	☺	☹
b)	The Earth's gravitational field strength varies in different places on Earth.	☺	☹
c)	An object will have a different mass on the Moon than on the Earth.	☺	☹
d)	Weight is caused by a gravitational field acting on a mass.	☺	☹

Q2   Two mad scientists are planning a **trip to Mars**.

a) Professor White tells Professor Brown —

> **"We won't need so much fuel for the return trip — the rocket will have less mass on Mars."**

Is Professor White's reasoning **correct**? Explain your answer.

....

b) Professor Brown wants to investigate **gravity** on Mars. He takes to Mars a small fire extinguisher which weighs **50 N** on Earth. He also takes his kitchen scales.

On Mars, Professor Brown weighs the fire extinguisher. The scales read **1.9 kg**. The gravitational field strength on Earth is 10 m/s². Calculate the gravitational field strength on Mars.

Find the mass of the fire extinguisher first.

1.90

....

....

....

Q3   A space probe lands on the icy surface of Europa, a moon of Jupiter. It weighs a set of **known masses**. The results are shown below.

Mass (kg)	0.1	0.2	0.3	0.4	0.5
Weight (N)	0.15	0.30	0.36	0.55	0.68

a) i) **Plot a graph** of this data on the axes given.

ii) Use your graph to estimate the **gravitational field strength** at Europa's surface.

....

....

b) Suggest why **several** masses were weighed, not just one.

....

Forces

Q1 A **teapot** sits on a table.

a) Explain why it **doesn't** sink into the table.

....

b) Jane picks up the teapot and hangs it from the ceiling by a **rope**.
What **vertical** forces now act on the teapot?

....

....

c) The rope **breaks** and the teapot **accelerates** towards the floor.

Are the vertical forces **balanced**? ....

Q2 A bear weighing **700 N** rides a bike at a **constant speed** with a driving force of **1500 N**.

a) Label the forces shown on the diagram.
Include the size of each force.

....

.... ◁= =▷ ....

b) The bear brakes and slows down.
In which direction is the resultant force?

....

....

Q3 Khaleeda helps Jenny investigate **falling objects**.
Jenny lets go of a beach ball and Khaleeda times how long it takes to fall.
Khaleeda draws the **distance-time** graph — it looks like the one shown.

Which phrase below describes points X, Y and Z?
Explain how you can tell this from the graph for each point.

forces in balance   **reaction force from ground acts**

unbalanced force of gravity

X: ....

You can tell this because: ....

Y: ....

You can tell this because: ....

Z: ....

You can tell this because: ....

Friction Forces and Terminal Speed

Q1 Use the words supplied to fill in the blanks in the paragraph below about a **sky-diver**.

decelerates	decrease	less	balances	increase	constant	greater	accelerates

When a sky-diver jumps out of a plane, his weight is .... than his

air resistance, so he .... downwards.

This causes his air resistance to .... until it .... his weight.

At this point, his velocity is ....

When his parachute opens, his air resistance is .... than his weight,

so he ....

This causes his air resistance to .... until it .... his weight.

Then his velocity is .... once again.

Q2 Which of the following will **not reduce the drag** force on an aeroplane?
Tick the appropriate box.

☐ flying higher (where the air is thinner)   ☐ carrying less cargo

☐ flying more slowly   ☐ making the plane more streamlined

Q3 Explain what is meant when an object is described as **streamlined**.

....

....

....

Q4 On the way down a slide, a penguin experiences **friction**.

a) Between which two surfaces is friction acting?

....

b) On the picture, draw an arrow to show the **direction**
in which friction is acting on the penguin.

c) Suggest how the penguin could **reduce** friction to speed up his slide.

....

....

Friction Forces and Terminal Speed

Q5   The graph shows how the velocity of a sky-diver
changes before and after he opens his **parachute**.

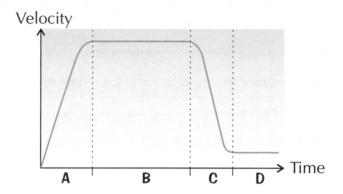

For each of the four regions A-D say whether the force of **weight** or
air resistance is greater, or if they are equal.

Region A: ....   Region B: ....

Region C: ....   Region D: ....

Q6   A scientist is investigating gravity by dropping a **hammer** and a **feather**.
Comment on the following predictions and explanations of what will happen.

  a) "They will land at the same time — gravity is the **same** for both."

....

....

....

  b) "The feather will reach its **terminal velocity** before the hammer."

....

....

....

Top Tips: Friction can be a bit of a nuisance but it's really useful too. Without it we wouldn't
be able to do loads of fun things like walk, run, do the locomotion (ask Kylie), or happily jump out of
planes at 4000 m with nothing but a bit of fabric to slow us down. Well, I say happily jump out
— I had to be pushed and was crying for my mummy all the way down. You live, you learn.

Module P3 — Forces for Transport

Forces and Acceleration

Q1   Use the words supplied to fill in the blanks. You may need to use some words **more than once**.

proportional	force	stationary	accelerates
constant	resultant	inversely	balanced

If the forces on an object are .... , it's either .... or

moving at .... speed. If an object has a .... force acting

on it, it .... in the direction of the .... The acceleration

is .... to the force and .... to its mass.

Q2   You're travelling home from school on a bus doing a **steady speed** in a **straight line**.
Which of the following is true? Tick the appropriate box.

☐ The driving force of the engine is bigger than friction and air resistance combined.

☐ There are no forces acting on the bus.

☐ The driving force of the engine is equal to friction and air resistance combined.

☐ No force is required to keep the bus moving.

Q3   A car tows a caravan along a road. At a constant speed, the pulling force of the car and the
opposing reaction force of the caravan are **equal**. Which statement correctly describes the
forces between the caravan and the car when the car **accelerates**? Tick the appropriate box.

☐ "The caravan's reaction force cancels out the pulling force of the car,
so the caravan won't accelerate."

☐ "The caravan's reaction force is at a right angle to the force pulling the car,
so the two forces don't affect one another."

☐ "The car's pulling force accelerates the caravan.
The caravan's reaction acts on the car, not the caravan."

Q4   Put these cars in order of **increasing driving force**.

Car	Mass (kg)	Maximum acceleration (m/s²)
Disraeli 9000	800	5
Palmerston 6i	1560	0.7
Heath TT	950	3
Asquith 380	790	2

1. ....

2. ....

3. ....

4. ....

Forces and Acceleration

Q5 Complete the statements below by **circling** the correct word(s).

> If there is **a balanced / an unbalanced** force acting on an object, it will accelerate in the
>
> **opposite / same** direction to/as the force. The size of the acceleration can be calculated
>
> using **F = m × a / F = m ÷ a**. This is **Newton's / Einstein's** 2nd law of **motion / physics**.

Q6 State whether or not the forces acting on the following items are **balanced**, and explain your reasoning.

a) A cricket ball slowing down as it rolls along the outfield.

....

....

b) A car going round a roundabout at a steady 30 mph.

....

....

c) A vase knocked off a window ledge.

....

....

d) A satellite orbiting over a fixed point on the Earth's surface.

....

....

e) A bag of rubbish ejected from a spacecraft in deep space.

....

....

Q7 Jo and Brian have fitted both their scooters with the **same engine**.
Brian and his scooter have a combined mass of **110 kg** and an acceleration of **2.80 m/s²**.
On her scooter, Jo only manages an acceleration of **1.71 m/s²**.

a) What **force** can the engine exert?

....

b) Calculate the combined **mass** of Jo and her scooter.

....

Forces and Acceleration

Q8   Tom drags a **1 kg mass** along a table with a newton-meter so that it accelerates at **0.25 m/s²**.
If the newton-meter reads **0.4 N**, what's the force of **friction** between the mass and the table?

....

....

....

The newton-meter shows the total force acting on the mass.

Q9   A camper van with a mass of **2500 kg** has a maximum driving force of **2650 N**.
It is driven along a straight, level road at a constant speed of **90 kilometres per hour**.
At this speed, air resistance is **2000 N** and the friction between the tyres and the road is **500 N**.

a)   **i)** What **force** is the engine exerting? ....

   ii) Complete the diagram to show all the forces acting on the camper van.
   Give the **size** of each force.

b)   A strong headwind begins blowing, with a force of **200 N**. The van slows down.
Calculate its **deceleration**.

....

c)   The driver notices that the van is slowing and puts his foot right down on the accelerator,
applying the **maximum** driving force. How does the acceleration of the camper van change?
(Assume that air resistance and friction remain at their previous values.)

....

....

....

Top Tips: A resultant force means your object will accelerate — it will change its speed
or direction (or both). But if your object has a constant speed (which could be zero) and a constant
direction, you can say with utter confidence that there ain't any resultant force. Be careful though —
a zero resultant force doesn't mean there are **no** forces, just that they all balance each other out.

Stopping Distances

Q1   The distance a car takes to stop is divided into: i) **thinking** distance and ii) **braking** distance.

a)   What is meant by 'braking distance'?

....

b)   Describe what is meant by 'thinking distance'.

....

....

c)   Why does a **tired** driver have a greater thinking distance?

....

Q2   Tick the boxes to show whether the following statements are **true** or **false**.

		True	False
a)	Tyres have a tread so they grip onto the water in wet weather.	☺	☹
b)	The braking distance will be the same for all road surfaces.	☺	☹
c)	The more heavily a car is loaded, the shorter its stopping distance.	☺	☹
d)	The total stopping distance is the thinking distance + the braking distance.	☺	☹

Q3   Will the following factors affect **thinking** distance, **braking** distance or **both**?
Write them in the relevant columns of the table.

Thinking Distance	Braking Distance

tiredness   alcohol

road surface   tyres

weather   brakes

speed   load

Q4   Tyres should have a minimum tread depth to stop the car **aquaplaning** in wet conditions. What is "aquaplaning" and why is it unsafe?

....

....

More on Stopping Distances

Q1   A car joins a motorway and **changes speed** from 30 mph to 60 mph.
Which one of the following statements is true? Tick the appropriate box.

☐ The total stopping distance will double.

☐ The braking distance will double.

☐ Thinking distance will double and braking distance will more than double.

☐ Both thinking and braking distance will more than double.

Q2   A car is travelling along a dry country road at **90 km/h**. The driver
sees a stop sign ahead of him and brakes. His thinking time is **0.6 s**.

You need to sort out the units for this question.

a)   Work out his thinking distance in **metres**.

....

b)   His braking distance is **18 car lengths**. His car is **3 m** long. How long does it take him to **stop**?

....

....

....

Q3   The **speed** of a vehicle affects thinking and braking distances **differently**.

a)   **i)**   What shape would a graph of thinking distance against speed be? Circle the correct answer.

   exponential   linear   squared   cubic   logarithmic

ii) Use the data in the table to
complete the graph on the right.

Speed (mph)	Thinking Distance (m)
20	6
40	12
60	18

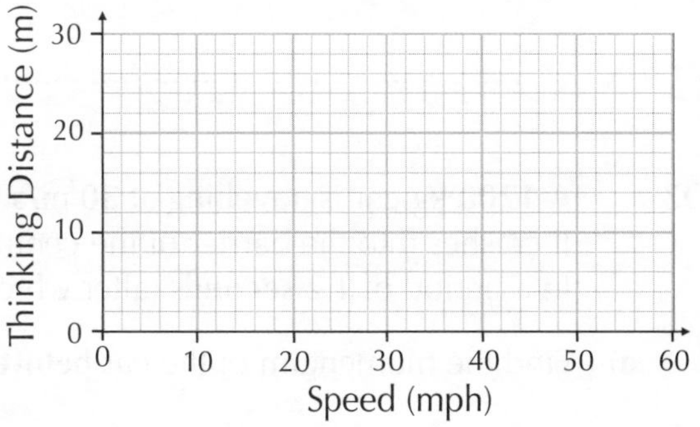

iii) Sketch another line on the same graph to show
how the thinking distance might change if the
driver had been drinking alcohol before driving.

b)   Complete the sentences below.

i) If the speed of a car is **doubled** the braking
distance is increased by a factor of ....

ii) If the speed of a car is **trebled** the braking
distance is increased by a factor of ....

c)   Use the graph on the right to find the braking
distance of a car travelling at 46 mph.
The braking distance is .... m

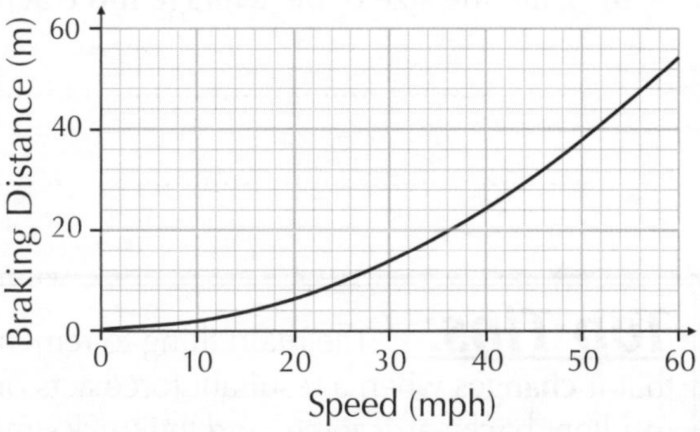

Momentum

Q1   Place the following four trucks in order of **increasing momentum**.

Truck A	Truck B	Truck C	Truck D
speed = 30 m/s	speed = 10 m/s	speed = 20 m/s	speed = 15 m/s
mass = 3000 kg	mass = 4500 kg	mass = 4000 kg	mass = 3500 kg

....

....

(lowest momentum)   .... , ... , ... , ...   (highest momentum)

Q2   A boat was travelling through the water in a straight line at constant speed.
A wave hit the side of the boat, exerting a resultant force of **8000 N** for **1.2 seconds**.

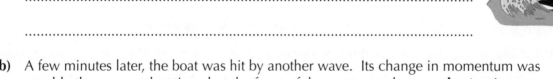

a)   Calculate the resulting change in the boat's **momentum**.

....

....

....

b)   A few minutes later, the boat was hit by another wave. Its change in momentum was
roughly the **same** as last time, but the force of the wave acted over a **shorter** time.
What does this tell you about the average force acting on the boat during the second wave?

....

Q3   A **1200 kg** car is travelling at **30 m/s** along the motorway.
It crashes into the barrier of the central reservation and is stopped
in a period of **1.2 seconds** (after which its momentum is zero).

a)   Find the momentum of the car **before** the crash.

....

b)   Find the size of the **average force** acting on the car as it stops.

....

....

Top Tips: The main thing to remember about momentum (apart from the equation) is
that it **changes** when a resultant force acts on an object. So if truck A started to brake, there'd be a
resultant backwards force, and the truck's momentum would decrease. Makes perfect sense really.

Car Safety

Q1 Since 1991 it has been **compulsory** in the UK for all adults
to wear **seat belts** in both the front and back seats of a car.

Explain how a seat belt **absorbs energy** to slow down a passenger when a crash occurs.

....

....

Q2 A car travels along a level road and **brakes** to avoid hitting a **giant statue of a cat**.
The car is fitted with a number of features that improve the **safety** of the car.

a) What type of **energy** does the moving car have?

....

b) The car **skids** and hits the cat statue. What safety feature could have **prevented** this?

....

c) Why are many car safety features designed to slow the car and its
occupants down over the **longest possible time** in a collision?

....

....

d) Building giant cat statues in the middle of the road is potentially dangerous.
Give **two** examples of safety features that can be **built on roads**.

1. ....

2. ....

Q3 The graph below shows the number of people killed in
motorway traffic accidents in the country of Thornland.

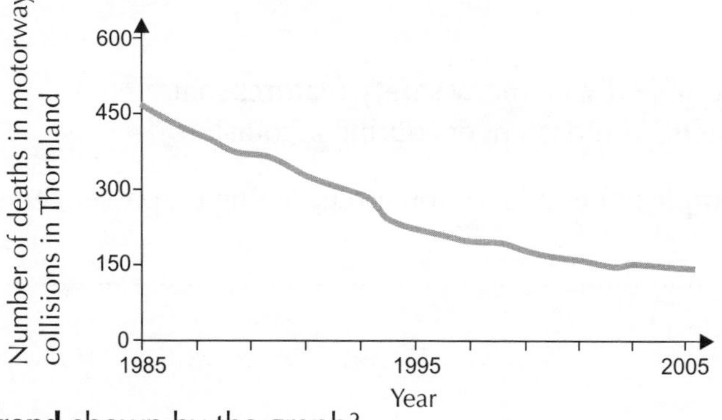

a) What is the overall **trend** shown by the graph?

....

b) Suggest a possible reason for this trend.

....

Car Safety

Q4 Complete this passage by using the words provided.

speeds	repeated		deaths		crashing	sized
	tested	data		dummies	sensors	

Safety features are .... to see how effectively they save lives or stop injuries in an accident. Test .... are gathered by .... cars containing crash test ...., both with and without safety features in place. They have .... at different places on their bodies to show where, and how badly, a real person would be injured. The tests are .... using different cars, at different ...., and using different .... dummies. The results are then compared with real data on .... and injuries from actual road accidents.

Q5 Two identical cars drive at the same speed down a dry road. One car is fitted with **ABS brakes**. Both cars brake heavily at the same time. The car without ABS **skids** before coming to a halt.

a) i) Describe how **ordinary** brakes can cause a car to skid.

....

ii) What do ABS brakes do that **prevents skidding**?

....

b) Give **one** other benefit of ABS brakes which can help to **prevent collisions**.

....

Q6 Modern cars are equipped with many **safety features** that reduce the **forces** acting on passengers during a collision.

a) Explain how a **crumple zone** reduces the forces acting on passengers during a collision.

....

....

b) Give two other car safety features that work in a similar way.

1. ....

2. ....

Work Done and Gravitational Potential Energy

Q1 Circle the **correct word** in each sentence to make them correct.

a) Work involves the transfer of **force** / **heat** / **energy**.

b) To do work a **force** / **current** acts over **a distance** / **time**.

c) Work is measured in **watts** / **joules**.

Q2 An elephant exerts a constant force of **1200 N** to push a donkey along a track at a steady **1 m/s**.

Calculate the work done by the elephant if the donkey moves **8 m**.

....

Q3 Tick the boxes to show whether the following statements are **true** or **false**.

		True	False
a)	Gravitational potential energy = mass × g × height.	☺	☹
b)	Work done is the energy possessed by an object due to height.	☺	☹
c)	On Earth, the gravitational field strength is approximately 10 N/kg.	☺	☹
d)	When a force moves an object, work is done.	☺	☹
e)	On Earth, a 3 kg chicken flies up 2.5 m to sit on a fence. It gains about 75 J of gravitational potential energy.	☺	☹

Q4 Jenny kicks a football, giving it **50 J** of energy.

a) How much **work** does Jenny do?

....

b) If Jenny kicks the ball with a force of **250 N**, over what **distance** does her kick act on the ball?

....

Q5 Shelagh keeps fit by cycling every day. She's calculated that she applies a steady force of **50 N** as she cycles. She decides to do at least **80 kJ** of work at each session.

a) What is the **minimum distance** Shelagh needs to cycle each session?

....

b) Shelagh says "For every 80 kJ of work I do moving the bike, I must be using up exactly 80 kJ of energy from my food." Is she right? Explain your answer.

....

....

Work Done and Gravitational Potential Energy

Q6 Explain why pushing your bicycle along a level road
means that you do some **work** in the scientific sense.

....

....

Q7 Dave works at a DIY shop. He has to load **28 flagstones** onto the delivery truck.
Each flagstone has a mass of **25 kg** and has to be lifted **1.2 m** onto the truck.

a) How much gravitational potential energy does **one** flagstone
gain when lifted onto the truck? (g = 10 m/s²)

....

....

b) What is the **total** gravitational potential energy gained by
the flagstones after they are all loaded onto the truck?

....

c) How much **work** does Dave do loading the truck?

....

....

Q8 Ben's weight is **600 N**. He climbs a ladder. The rungs of the ladder are **20 cm** apart.

a) What force is Ben doing work **against** as he climbs?

....

b) How much work does Ben do when he climbs **10 rungs**?
(Ignore any 'wasted' energy.)

....

....

*Don't forget to think
about the underlined units.*

c) How many rungs of the ladder must Ben climb before he
has done **15 kJ** of work? (Ignore any 'wasted' energy.)

....

....

Top Tips: The main thing to remember here is that energy transferred and work done are the
same thing. You're bound to get asked to do a calculation, so make sure you know the equations and
how to use them. All work questions are pretty similar — just keep practising and you'll be fine.

Module P3 — Forces for Transport

Kinetic Energy

Q1   Find the **kinetic energy** of a **200 kg** tiger running at a speed of **9 m/s**.

....

....

Q2   A **golf ball** is hit and given **9 J** of kinetic energy.
The ball's speed is **20 m/s**. What is its **mass**?

....

....

Q3   A **60 kg** skydiver jumps out of an aeroplane and free-falls.
Find the skydiver's **speed** if she has **90 750 J** of kinetic energy.

....

....

Q4   A car of mass **1000 kg** travels at **10 m/s**.

a)   What is its kinetic energy?

....

b)   Decide if the following statements are **true** or **false**.

	True	False
Kinetic energy is energy due to movement.	☺	☹
If a driver doubles her speed, her braking distance will be twice as far.	☺	☹
If the mass of a car is doubled, the braking distance will double.	☺	☹
Brakes convert kinetic energy into mostly heat energy to slow down a car.	☺	☹

Q5   A large truck and a car both have a kinetic energy of **614 400 J**.
The mass of the truck is **12 288 kg** and the car **1200 kg**.

a)   Calculate the speed of:

i) the car ....

ii) the truck ....

b)   John is playing with his remote-controlled toy car and truck.
The car's mass is **100 g**. The truck's mass is **300 g**.
The car is moving **twice as fast** as the truck.
Which has more kinetic energy — the car or the truck? Explain your answer.

....

....

Falling Objects and Roller Coasters

Q1 A toy cricket ball hit straight upwards has a gravitational potential energy of **9 J** at the top of its flight.

Assume that there's no air resistance.

a) What is the ball's **kinetic energy** just before it hits the ground?

....

b) Calculate the **speed** of the ball at this time if its mass is **100 g**.

....

c) What **height** did the ball fall from? $g = 10 \text{ m/s}^2$

....

Q2 A roller coaster and passengers are **stationary** at the top of a ride. At this point they have a gravitational potential energy of **300 kJ**.

a) Draw lines to connect the correct energy statement with each stage of the roller coaster.

K.E. = Kinetic energy
G.P.E. = gravitational potential energy

A   **minimum P.E., maximum K.E.**

B   **K.E. is being converted to P.E.**

C   **maximum P.E.**

D   **P.E. is being converted to K.E.**

b) **i)** When the roller coaster is at **half** its original height, how much kinetic energy should it have?

....

ii) Explain why in real life the kinetic energy is **less** than this.

....

Q3 Jo is sitting at the top of a helter-skelter ride and her mass is **50 kg**.

$g = 10 \text{ m/s}^2$

a) If her gravitational potential energy is **4000 J**, how high up is Jo?

....

b) She comes down the helter-skelter and at the bottom her kinetic energy is **1500 J**. How much energy has been '**wasted**' coming down the ride?

....

c) Which **force** causes this energy to be wasted? ....

d) Jo designs a new helter-skelter where **no energy is wasted**.

She wants to be travelling at **8.6 m/s** at the end of the ride.
How tall does her helter-skelter need to be?

....

Power

Q1 Complete this passage by using the words provided.

heat	energy	one hundred	rate	light	watts	joules

Power is the .... of doing work, or how much .... is

transferred per second. It is measured in .... or ....

per second. A 100 W light bulb transfers .... joules of electrical

energy into .... and .... each second.

Q2 George drives to work every day in a small car with a power of **50 kW**.

a) If the journey takes **5 minutes**, how much energy does the car get from its fuel?

....

b) One day George's car breaks down and so he cycles to work. The journey takes him
12 minutes and he transfers **144 kJ** of energy. What is his power?

....

Q3 Catherine and Sally decide to have a race to see who can get to the ice cream van first.
Catherine won the race in **6.2 s**, while Sally took **6.4 s**. They both did **1200 J** of work.

a) How much **power** did each girl deliver?

....

....

....

b) Catherine and Sally have another race, this time they race up a set of stairs. At the top of the stairs,
Catherine has a gravitational potential energy (G.P.E.) of **2400 J**, and Sally has a G.P.E. of **2300 J**.

Sally won the race in **3.9 s**, while Catherine took **4.1 s**. Which girl delivered more **power**?

....

....

Q4 A sports car transfers **2 650 000 kJ** of chemical energy
per hour into kinetic energy. Calculate its power output.

*You need to change the units
into <u>joules</u> and <u>seconds</u>.*

....

....

....

Power

Q5 Josie runs home after school so she can watch her favourite TV programme.

    a) For the first **24 m** of the run she exerts a force of **88 N** over **6 s**.
Calculate her power for this part of her run.

....

....

    b) Josie gets to her house and runs up the stairs to her room. She weighs **600 N** and runs at **0.8 m/s**.
How much power does she deliver getting up the stairs?

....

Q6 Tom likes to build model boats. His favourite boat
is the Carter, which has a motor power of **150 W**.

    a) How much energy does the Carter transfer in **10 minutes**?

....

    b) The petrol for the boat's motor can supply **30 kJ/ml**.
What volume of petrol is used up in **10 minutes**?

....

    c) Tom decides to get a model speed boat which transfers **120 kJ** in the same 10 minute journey.
What is the power of the engine?

....

Q7 Andy is developing a new racing car. He knows that at **130 km/h** the car exerts
a driving force of **3200 N** and wants to calculate the **power** of the engine.

    a) Andy borrows a physics book from the library and finds **three equations**:

$$\text{Speed} = \frac{\text{Distance}}{\text{Time}} \qquad \text{Work done} = \text{Force} \times \text{Distance} \qquad \text{Power} = \frac{\text{Work done}}{\text{Time}}$$

Show how he can use these equations to form an equation for power in terms of **speed** and **force**.

....

....

....

    b) Calculate the power of the racing car's engine in **kW**. Give your answer to the nearest kW.

....

....

Fuel Consumption and Emissions

Q1 Complete this passage by using some of the words provided.

braking	slower	mgh	heavier	mass	acceleration
½mv²	lighter	fuel	speed	faster	height

To move a car, the energy from the .... needs to be changed into kinetic

energy (K.E.). Since K.E. = ... the higher the .... of the

car or the .... it travels, the higher the K.E. will be and the more energy

you need from fuel to give it that K.E.

Q2 A car's fuel consumption is **3.4 l/100 km**. How much
fuel is used in a **250 km** journey? Tick the correct box.

☐ 3.4 l   ☐ 8.5 l   ☐ 6.8 l   ☐ 10.0 l

Q3 The **fuel consumption** of a car can vary.

a) Explain how different **driving styles** affect the fuel consumption of a car.

....

....

....

b) How does fuel consumption vary with the **speed** of a car?

....

....

Q4 The table below shows the **CO$_2$ emissions** and **fuel consumption** from four different cars.

Car	CO$_2$ Emissions (g/km)	Fuel Consumption (mpg)
Trygve XXL	139	42
Waldheim 4.1	345	19
Boutros GTI	227	28
Annan 97eco	181	45

a) Which car has the **lowest value** of fuel consumption if measured in **l/100 km**? ....

b) i) What **trend** can you identify between fuel consumption and CO$_2$ emissions from this data?

....

ii) Suggest **one** reason why this trend isn't followed by every car.

....

Fuels for Cars

Q1   Tick the boxes to show whether the following statements are **true** or **false**.

                                                                                       True   **False**

    a) Biofuels are made from plants and organic waste.

    b) Biofuels don't give off any carbon dioxide when they're burnt.

    c) Pollution is created in the production of cars that run on biofuels.

    d) Biofuels are non-renewable.

    e) Burning biofuels produces more pollution overall that burning fossil fuels.

Q2   Petrol is made from oil, which is a **fossil fuel**.

    a) Are fossil fuels renewable or non-renewable?

    ....

    b) Give two **environmental problems** that burning fossil fuels in cars can cause.

        1. ....

        2. ....

    c) Give an example of an '**alternative fuel**' to petrol and diesel. ....

Q3   Trevor's car has **two engines**, a normal **petrol** engine and an **electric** motor.
He uses the electric motor for short journeys but uses the petrol engine for longer drives.

    a) How does using the electric motor cause **less damage** to the environment at the point of use?

    ....

    b) Explain why Trevor has to use the **petrol** engine for longer journeys.

    ....

    ....

    c) The electric motor is powered by **batteries** that need to be frequently charged from a **mains supply**.
If Trevor always used the electric motor, would his driving have any impact on the environment?
Explain your answer.

    ....

    ....

    ....

    d) Trevor fits his car with solar panels so he can charge the batteries using energy from the Sun.
Do solar panels produce **any** pollution? Explain your answer.

    ....

    ....

Mixed Questions — Module P3

Q1   Jack and Jill go up a hill to go on a roller coaster. With them in it, the roller coaster carriage has a total mass of **1200 kg**.

   a)   What is the **weight** of the carriage? (Assume g = 10 m/s².) ....

   b)   At the start of the ride the carriage rises up to its highest point of **34 m** above the ground and stops. Calculate its gain in gravitational potential energy.

      ....

   c)   The carriage then falls to a **third** of its maximum height. Assuming there is no air resistance or friction, calculate the speed of the carriage at this point.

      ....

      ....

      ....

   d)   At the end of the ride, the carriage slows down, decelerating at **6.4 m/s²**. How long does it take the carriage to slow down from **20 m/s** and come to a stop?

      ....

      ....

Q2   Cherie robs a bank and escapes in a getaway car with a mass of **2100 kg**. She travels at a constant speed of **90 km/h** along a straight, level road.

   a)   Calculate the **kinetic energy** of the car.

      ....

   b)   Is there a **resultant force** on the car? Explain your answer.

      ....

   c)   A police car swings into the middle of the road and stops ahead of Cherie's car. Cherie brakes with a reaction time of **0.7 s** and a braking time of **3.2 s**.

     i)   Give two factors that could have affected her reaction time.

       1. ....

       2. ....

     ii) What happens to the kinetic energy of the car as Cherie **slows down**?

       ....

   d)   The getaway car has **ABS brakes**. How would you expect having ABS brakes to influence Cherie's braking distance?

      ....

Mixed Questions — Module P3

Q3 In the film 'Crouching Sparrow, Hidden Beaver', a **95 kg** dummy is dropped **60 m** from the top of a building. (Assume that g = 10 m/s².)

a) Sketch a **distance-time** graph and a **velocity-time** graph for the dummy from the moment it is dropped until just after it hits the ground. (Ignore air resistance and assume the dummy does not reach a terminal speed.)

distance from top of tower ↑ → time

velocity ↑ → time

b) Do any **forces** act on the dummy when it lies still **on the ground** (after falling)? If so, what are they?

....

c) The take doesn't go to plan so the dummy is lifted back to the top of the building using a motor.

i) How much **work** is done on the dummy to get it to the top of the building?

....

ii) The useful power output of the motor is **760 W**. How long does it take to get the dummy to the top of the building?

....

Q4 A sky-diver jumps out of an aeroplane. Her weight is **700 N**.

a) What force causes her to **accelerate** downwards?

....

b) After **10 s** she is falling at a steady speed of **60 m/s**. State the force of air resistance that is acting on her.

....

c) She now opens her parachute, which increases the air resistance to **2000 N**. Explain what happens immediately after she **opens the parachute**.

....

....

d) After falling with her parachute open for 5 s, the sky-diver is travelling at a steady speed of **4 m/s**. What is the **air resistance** force now?

....

Estimating Population Sizes

Q1 Some students wanted to estimate the size of the **population of clover plants** around their school.

a) Explain the difference between a population and a community.

....

....

b) The school field is 250 m long by 180 m wide. Hannah counted 11 clover plants in a 1 m² area of the field. Approximately how many clover plants are there likely to be on the whole field?

....

c) Lisa decided to collect data from five different 1 m² areas of the school field. Her results are shown in the table below.

	Area 1	Area 2	Area 3	Area 4	Area 5
No. of plants	11	9	8	9	7

i) What was the **average** number of clover plants per m² in Lisa's survey?

....

ii) Use Lisa's data to estimate the population size of clover plants on the field.

....

d) Whose estimation of population size is likely to be more accurate? Explain your answer.

....

....

Q2 In a capture-recapture experiment, there were **30** animals in both the first and second samples. **Seven** of the animals in the second sample were marked.

a) Estimate the population size using the formula in the box below.

$$\text{Population Size} = \frac{\text{number in first sample} \times \text{number in second sample}}{\text{number in second sample previously marked}}$$

....

....

b) Give three **assumptions** that you have to make when you're using capture-recapture data to estimate population size.

1. ....

2. ....

3. ....

72

Ecosystems and Distribution of Organisms

Q1 a) Circle the correct definition of the word '**ecosystem**' from the choices below.

> The place where an organism lives.

> All the organisms living in a particular area.

> All the organisms living in a particular area, as well as all the non-living (abiotic) conditions.

b) Explain the difference between a **habitat** and an **ecosystem**.

....

....

c) Ecosystems are often described as being '**self-supporting**' apart from their energy source. Explain what this means.

....

....

Q2 a) Taylor is studying the **distribution** of two species of moss across the school playground. Describe how he could carry out a **transect** with **quadrats** to help with his investigation.

....

....

Taylor draws the following **kite diagram** from the results of his transect:

b) Describe the distribution of **species 2** along the transect.

....

....

Zonation

Q1 The distribution of organisms can be affected by **abiotic factors**.

a) Explain what is meant by the term '**abiotic factors**'.

....

b) List **three** abiotic factors that could affect the distribution of an organism.

....

....

Q2 Molly is doing a science project on **zonation** along the coastline near her town.

a) Explain what is meant by the term '**zonation**'.

....

b) Molly draws a sketch of what she finds on one particular section of the shore and marks on some observations about the abiotic conditions at the bottom.

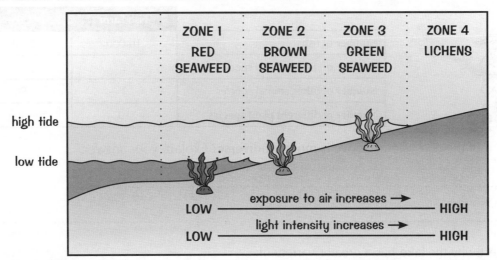

i) Which organism from the diagram would you expect to be **least tolerant** to low light intensity? Explain your answer.

....

....

ii) Using Molly's sketch and her observations about light intensity and exposure to air, suggest why there is more **brown seaweed** in zone 2 than in zone 1.

....

....

Top Tips: If you get a zonation question in the exam, don't panic. Just remember to think about the abiotic factors involved and how they might affect where different organisms are found.

Biodiversity

Q1 What is '**biodiversity**' a measure of? Underline **three** correct statements from the list below.

The number of different species in an area.

The variation in abiotic factors in an area.

The number of different habitats in an area.

The amount of variation between individuals of the same species in an area.

The number of individuals of one species in an area.

Q2 Fish farms are **artificial ecosystems**.

a) What is the key difference between a natural ecosystem and an artificial ecosystem?

....

....

The table below shows data for a fish farm and a natural lake.

	Fish Farm	Lake
Number of fish	10 000	3 000
Number of different fish species	1	15
Number of other animal species	3	50
Number of different plant species	10	50

b) Which of the ecosystems above is **more biodiverse**? Explain your answer.

....

....

c) Suggest why the **lake** has a greater variety of:

i) animal species ....

....

ii) plant species ....

....

Q3 Explain why **forestry plantations** are less biodiverse than **natural woodlands**.

....

....

....

Photosynthesis

Q1   Complete the chemical equation for photosynthesis.

$$6CO_2 + \text{.............................} \xrightarrow[\text{chlorophyll}]{\text{LIGHT}} C_6H_{12}O_6 + \text{.............................}$$

Q2   Complete the sentences below by circling the correct word(s) from each pair.

  a) Photosynthesis is a **three** / **two** stage process.

  b) Photosynthesis takes place in the **chloroplasts** / **nucleus** of plant cells.

  c) First, light energy is used to split **water** / **carbon dioxide** into oxygen gas and hydrogen ions.

  d) Then **oxygen gas** / **carbon dioxide gas** combines with the hydrogen ions
     to make glucose and water.

Q3   New potato plants are grown from potato **tubers**, which contain stores of **insoluble starch**.

  a) Suggest how the new plants obtain the energy needed for growth.

    ....

  b) Suggest why the plants no longer need this energy source once they have grown above the soil.

    ....

  c) Give **two** reasons why the tubers store glucose as **insoluble starch**.

    ....

    ....

Q4   Complete the passage about **glucose** by choosing the correct words from the list below.

proteins	lipids	walls	convert	leaves	energy	cellulose

Plants make glucose in their .... Some of it is used for respiration,

which releases .... and allows the plant to ....

the rest of the glucose into other substances. In rapidly growing plants, glucose is

converted into .... to build cell ....

Some glucose is combined with nitrates from the soil to make amino acids and

.................................., which are used for growth and repair. Glucose can also be

turned into .... for storage in seeds.

Understanding Photosynthesis

Q1   Scientists have been studying plant growth for centuries.

Describe the view of **early Greek scientists** on how plants grow and gain mass.

....

....

Q2   In the mid-1600s **Jan van Helmont** carried out an experiment to investigate how plants gain mass. He planted a willow tree in some soil and left it for 5 years, adding only water to the soil.

a)   Describe the results of van Helmont's experiment.

....

....

b)   What conclusion did van Helmont draw from these results?

....

c)   Explain how van Helmont's experiment helped our understanding of photosynthesis.

....

....

Q3   Miss Webb's biology class are recreating some of **Joseph Priestley's** famous experiments.

a)   They place a lit candle in a sealed container and leave it until it goes out. Describe what you would expect to happen when they try to re-light the candle in the sealed container.

....

b)   The class carry out the experiment again. This time they place a green plant in the container along with the candle. Describe what you would expect to happen when they try to re-light the candle in a week's time.

....

c)   Explain your answer to part **b)**.

....

....

More on Photosynthesis

Q1 Below are some straightforward questions about **limiting factors**.

a) List **three** factors that can limit the rate of photosynthesis.

....

....

b) Explain the meaning of the term "limiting factor".

....

Q2 Jacquie was growing some herbs in her kitchen. Changes taking place in her kitchen that affect the rate of photosynthesis are shown in the table below.

Change in conditions	Environmental factor(s) changed	Effect on photosynthesis
A cooling fan is turned on.		
More plants are added to the room.		
Jacquie's family enter the room.		
An electric heater is switched on.		
A light bulb is switched on.		
The blinds are closed and lights switched off.		

a) For each statement, identify which environmental factor (or factors) will have changed — **carbon dioxide**, **temperature** or **light**. Write your answers in the table.

b) Predict the effect of each change on the rate of photosynthesis by choosing from **increase, decrease** or **no effect.** Write your answers in the table.

Q3 Describe how scientists used **isotopes** to work out whether the **oxygen** produced in photosynthesis came from carbon dioxide or water.

....

....

....

More on Photosynthesis

Q4 Richard grows house plants **commercially** for sale to garden centres. Over the years Richard has spent a lot of money building **glasshouses** in which to grow his plants.

a) Richard **burns fuel** in his glasshouses to increase the air temperature, making his plants grow faster. Burning the fuel also releases carbon dioxide.

i) Describe the effect of increasing the air temperature on the rate of photosynthesis.

....

....

ii) Suggest why the carbon dioxide released by the fuel makes the plants **grow faster**.

....

b) Richard's glasshouses also have **artificial lighting**.

i) **When** would Richard use the artificial lighting?

....

ii) Suggest a **benefit** of providing artificial lighting.

....

Q5 Average daytime summer temperatures in different habitats are recorded in the table below.

Area of the world	Temperature (°C)
Forest	19
Arctic	0
Desert	32
Grassland	22
Rainforest	27

a) Plot a **bar chart** for these results on the grid.

b) From the values for temperature, in which area would you expect fewest plants to grow?

....

c) Suggest a reason for your answer.

....

....

Diffusion

Q1 Complete the passage below by circling the correct word in each pair.

> Diffusion is the **direct / net** movement of particles from an area of **higher / lower** concentration
> to an area of **higher / lower** concentration. It's caused by the **uniform / random** movement of
> individual particles. The rate of diffusion is faster when the concentration gradient is
> **bigger / smaller**. It is slower when there is a **large / small** distance over which diffusion occurs
> and when there is **more / less** surface area for diffusion to take place across.

Q2 The first diagram below shows a **cup of water** which has just had a **drop of dye** added.

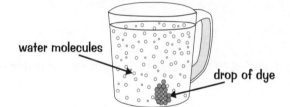 

water molecules

drop of dye

a) In the second cup above, draw the molecules of **dye** in the water after an hour.

b) Predict how the rate of diffusion of the dye would change if a large drop of dye was used rather
than a small drop of dye.

....

c) Explain the movement of the dye molecules in terms of differences in concentration.

....

....

Q3 Patsy was studying in her bedroom. Her dad was cooking curry for tea in
the kitchen. Soon Patsy could smell the curry that her dad was making.

a) Her dad was warm so he switched on a fan. Suggest what effect the
fan would have on the rate that the curry particles spread through the house.

....

b) After tasting the curry, Patsy's dad added more curry powder. What effect would this
have on the smell of the curry? Explain your answer using the word **concentration**.

....

....

Diffusion

Q4 Some statements about **diffusion** are written below.
Decide which are correct and then write **true** or **false** in the spaces.

a) Diffusion takes place in all types of substances. ....

b) Large protein molecules can diffuse across cell membranes. ....

c) Diffusion happens more quickly when there is a higher concentration gradient. ....

d) A larger surface area makes diffusion happen more quickly. ....

e) When there is a larger distance for particles to travel across, ...
the rate of diffusion is faster.

Q5 Two diagrams of diffusion are shown below.

Would you expect the molecules to diffuse from left to right across the membrane **faster** in situation A or B? Explain your answer.

....

....

Q6 Phil was investigating the diffusion of **glucose** (a small molecule) and **starch** (a large molecule) through a **membrane**. He placed equal amounts of glucose solution and starch solution inside a bag designed to act like a cell membrane. He then put the bag into a beaker of water.

a) After an hour, Phil tested the water for the presence of starch and glucose. Circle which of the following you would expect to be found in the water outside the bag:

glucose   **starch**

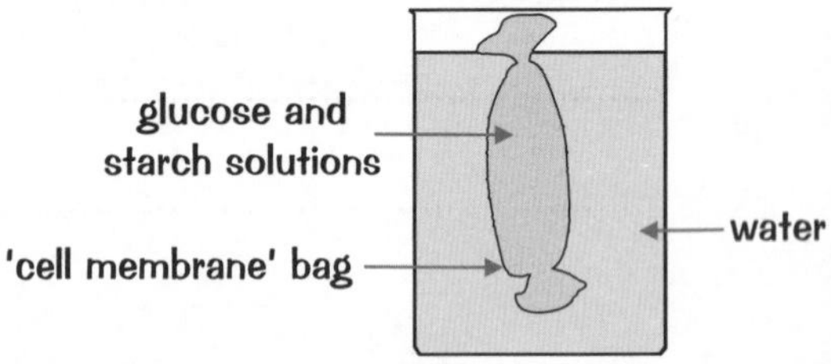

b) Explain your answer to part **a)**.

....

....

c) Phil did the experiment again using the same amounts of glucose and starch solutions. This time he used a much longer, thinner bag.

Will the diffusion happen faster or more slowly this time? Explain your answer.

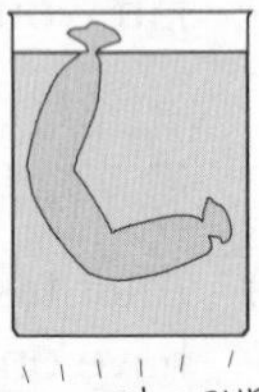

....

Think about the surface areas of the bags.

....

Top Tips: Don't forget — diffusing molecules aren't all heading directly towards areas of lower concentration. They're all moving randomly, which makes them spread out evenly after a while.

Leaves and Diffusion

Q1   Name the parts labelled **A – E** to complete the diagram of a **leaf** below.

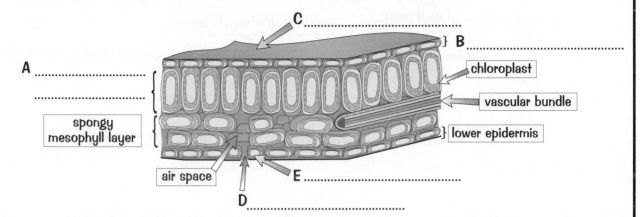

Q2   Answer the following questions about **gas exchange** in leaves.

a)   Which process in the leaf uses CO_2 and produces O_2? ....

b)   Which process in the leaf uses O_2 and produces CO_2? ....

Q3   Jill decides to do an experiment with her new fish tank before she puts the fish in.

She puts some **aquatic plants** in the tank and places it by the window. She then measures the concentration of **carbon dioxide** in the water over a period of 24 hours. She plots a graph of her results.

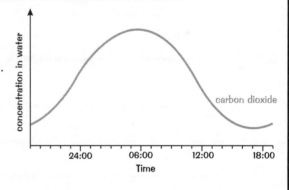

a)   What **process** causes the carbon dioxide concentration to increase between 19:00, when Jill started the experiment, and 05:00?

....

b)   Why do the plants need to carry out this process all the time?

....

c)   Explain why the carbon dioxide concentration falls between 06:00 and 17:00.

....

d)   Jill also measures the **oxygen** concentration in the water. Sketch another line on the graph to show how you would expect the oxygen concentration to change during Jill's experiment.

e)   Explain your answer to part **d)**.

....

....

82

Leaves and Photosynthesis

Q1   Draw lines to match up the following **features** of a leaf with how they help with **photosynthesis**.

air spaces in mesophyll layer   short diffusion distance

broad leaves   control when stomata open and close for gas exchange

guard cells   large surface area exposed to light

thin leaves   large internal surface area for gas exchange

Q2   Complete the following passage by choosing the correct words from the list below.

transport	support	straw	vascular	blood	xylem

Leaves contain a network of .... bundles. These are the phloem

and .... vessels. They .... water and glucose

to and from the leaf, as well as helping to .... the leaf structure.

Q3   Name three different **photosynthetic pigments** found in plants.

1. ....

2. ....

3. ....

Q4   Explain how the following features make leaves well adapted to **absorb light** for photosynthesis.

a)   different photosynthetic pigments

....

b)   most chloroplasts arranged in the palisade layer

....

c)   a transparent upper epidermis

....

Module B4 — It's a Green World

Osmosis

Q1   Fill in the missing words to complete the paragraph.

diffusion	higher	water	lower	membrane	random	partially

Osmosis is the movement of .... molecules across a ....
permeable .... from a region of .... water concentration
(a dilute solution) to a region of .... water concentration
(a concentrated solution). Osmosis is a special type of .... and is a
consequence of the .... movement of individual water molecules.

Q2   Look at the diagram and answer the questions below.

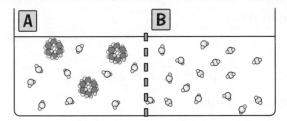
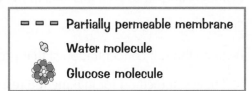

a)   On which side of the membrane is there the highest concentration of water molecules? ....

b)   What is a **partially permeable membrane**?

....

c)   Predict whether the level of liquid on side B will **rise** or **fall**. Explain your answer.

....

....

Q3   A **red blood cell** is in some very **dilute** blood plasma.

a)   Will water move into or out of the cell? Explain your answer.

....

....

Learning by osmosis

b) i)   Describe what happens to an animal cell if it **takes in** too much water, and give the technical
term for it.

....

ii)   Describe what happens to an animal cell if it **loses** too much water, and give the technical
term for it.

....

Osmosis

Q4   Some **potato cylinders** were placed in solutions of different **salt concentrations**. At the start of the experiment each cylinder was 50 mm long. Their final lengths are recorded in the table below.

Concentration of salt solution (molar)	Length of potato cylinder (mm)	Change in length of potato cylinder (mm)
0.0	60	
0.5	56	
1.0	50	
1.5	34	
2.0	45	

a)   Plot a bar chart showing salt concentration and the final length of the potato cylinders.

b)   Work out the change in length of each of the cylinders and write your answers in the table above.

c)   Study the pattern of the results.

   i)   State the salt concentration(s) that produced unexpected results.   ....

   ii) Suggest a method for making the results more reliable.

   ....

d)   Suggest **three** factors that should have remained constant to ensure that this was a fair test.

   ....

   ....

Q5   Plant cells look different depending on how much **water** they contain.

a)   Use the words in the box below to describe the states of the following cells.

plasmolysed	turgid	normal	flaccid

A ....   B ....   C ....   D ....

b)   Explain why plants start to wilt if they don't have enough water.

   ....

   ....

c)   Explain why the cell in diagram D hasn't totally lost its shape.

   ....

Transport Systems in Plants

Q1   Put the following statements under the **correct heading** in the table.

transport water

made of living cells

transport substances up the stem

transport substances both up
and down the stem

transport food

made of dead cells

Xylem vessels	Phloem vessels

Q2   The diagram shows a cross-section of a **leaf**.

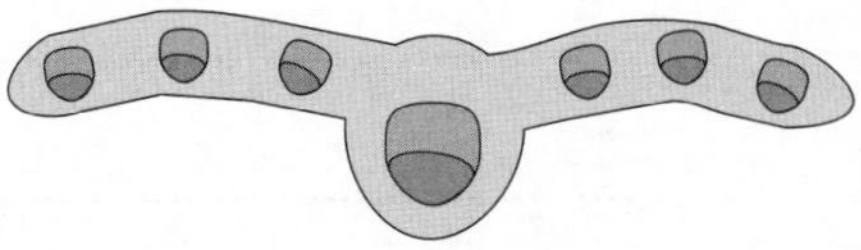

a) Label a **xylem vessel**, and a **phloem vessel** on the diagram.

b) Circle a **vascular bundle** on the diagram.

Q3   The diagram shows a cross-section of a **plant's stem**.

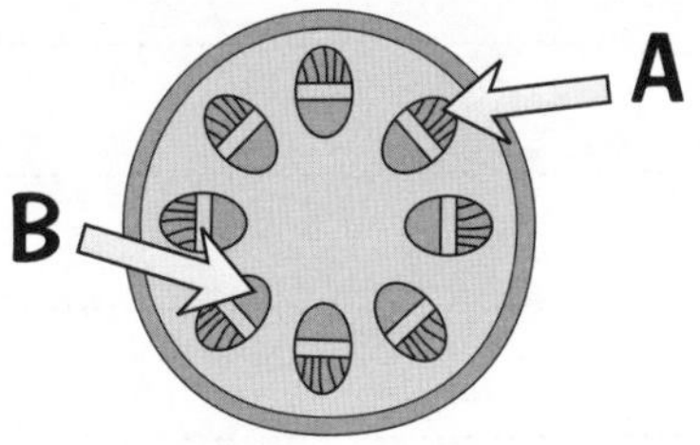

a) Name parts A and B.

A = ...

B = ...

b) Describe the function of **A** in the stem.

....

c) Describe one way that a cross-section of a root would look different from
the cross-section of a stem.

....

Q4   Answer the following questions about **xylem**.

a) Name **two** substances transported by the xylem.   ....

b) Describe the structure of a xylem tube.

....

....

Module B4 — It's a Green World

Water Flow Through Plants

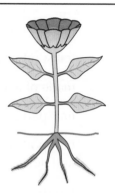

Q1   Complete this diagram of a **plant** according to the instructions given below.

  a)   Put an **X** on the diagram to show one place where water enters the plant.

  b)   Add a **Y** to the diagram to show one place where water leaves the plant.

  c)   Add arrows to the diagram to show how water moves from where it enters to where it leaves.

Q2   **Root hair cells** are found on the roots of plants.

  a)   Draw a diagram of a root hair cell in the box provided.

  b)   Describe how water is drawn into this cell.

    ....

    ....

Q3   Give four ways that transpiration **benefits** plants.

    1. ....

    2. ....

    3. ....

    4. ....

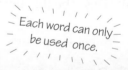

Each word can only be used once.

Q4   Choose from the following words to complete the passage.

leaves	evaporation	roots	flowers	photosynthesis
phloem	diffusion	transpiration	xylem	stem

Most water leaves plants through the .... by the processes of

.... and .... of water vapour. This creates a slight

shortage of water in the ...., which draws water from the rest of the

plant through the .... vessels. This causes more water to be drawn up

from the .... This whole process is called ....

It's a side effect of the way leaves are adapted for ....

Water Flow Through Plants

Q5   Indicate whether each of the following statements is **true** or **false**.

                                                                                    True False

a)   The transpiration rate decreases as the temperature increases.

b)   The more intense the light, the faster the transpiration rate.

c)   Transpiration happens more slowly when the air is humid.

d)   As the wind speed increases, the rate of transpiration decreases.

Q6   Explain the effect of increasing **temperature** on **transpiration rate**.

....

....

Q7   Plants need to **balance** water loss with water gain.

a)   Give two ways that plants are adapted to reduce water loss from their leaves.

1. ....

2. ....

b)   Suggest one way plants in hot climates adapted to reduce water loss.

Hint: Think about the stomata.

....

Q8   The diagram shows an **open stoma** and a **closed stoma**.

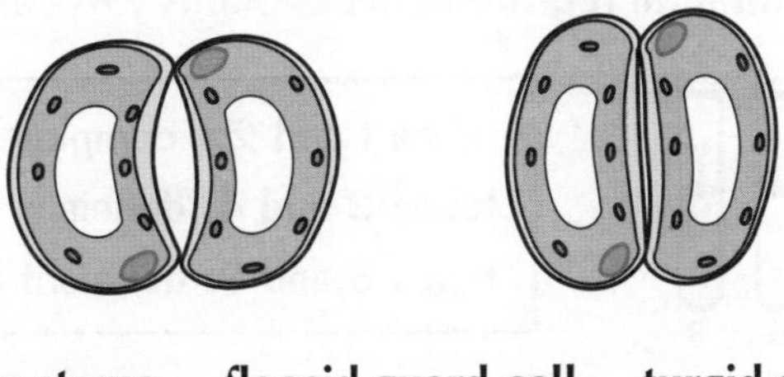

a)   Label the following: **open stoma**,   **flaccid guard cell**,   **turgid guard cell**,   **closed stoma**

b)   Circle the correct word(s) in each pair to complete the sentences below.

i)   When the guard cells are **turgid / flaccid** the stoma opens.

ii) The stoma closes when the guard cells are **turgid / flaccid**.

iii) Stomata **open / close** at night and when water supply is **high / low**.

c)   Would you expect a plant's stomata to be open or closed on a bright sunny morning? Explain your answer.

....

....

Minerals Needed for Healthy Growth

Q1   Draw lines to match the following **minerals** with their **functions** in plants.

MAGNESIUM		for making amino acids and proteins
NITRATES		for making chlorophyll
PHOSPHATES		for making DNA and cell membranes
POTASSIUM		for helping enzymes to function

Q2   Spring has arrived but Pat has noticed that his **tomato crop** is **not** growing well and the plants have yellow older leaves.

a)   Suggest a cause of both the poor plant growth and yellow older leaves.

....

b)   Pat has been offered some **manure** for his field. The table shows the mineral content of different manures.

Which type of manure would you recommend Pat use? Explain your answer.

....

....

Material	% Nitrogen	% Phosphorus	% Potassium
Bullock manure	0.6	0.1	0.7
Cow manure	0.4	0.1	0.4
Horse manure	0.6	0.1	0.5
Pig manure	0.4	0.1	0.5
Poultry manure	1.0	0.4	0.6
Sheep manure	0.8	0.1	0.7

Q3   An investigation into the **mineral requirements** of plants was carried out as shown below.

tubes 1 and 2:   complete mineral supply
tubes 3 and 4: deficient in phosphates
tubes 5 and 6: deficient in magnesium

a)   Suggest why tubes 1 and 2 were included.

....

b)   Predict how the seedlings in the following tubes will grow:

i) 3 and 4 ....

ii) 5 and 6 ....

c)   Suggest why a sufficient amount of all the minerals except one was supplied to tubes 3, 4, 5 and 6.

....

....

Minerals Needed for Healthy Growth

Q4 Natalie measures the **magnesium** level in the soil in her orchard every year. The graph below shows how the magnesium level in the soil changed over the ten year period from 2000 to 2010.

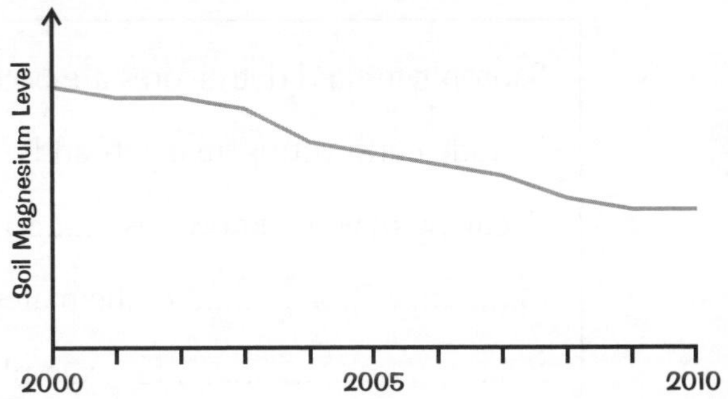

a) Describe the general trend shown in the magnesium level over the ten year period.

....

b) What do plants need magnesium for?

....

....

c) How could Natalie identify plants **deficient** in magnesium?

....

....

Q5 A diagram of a **specialised plant cell** is shown.

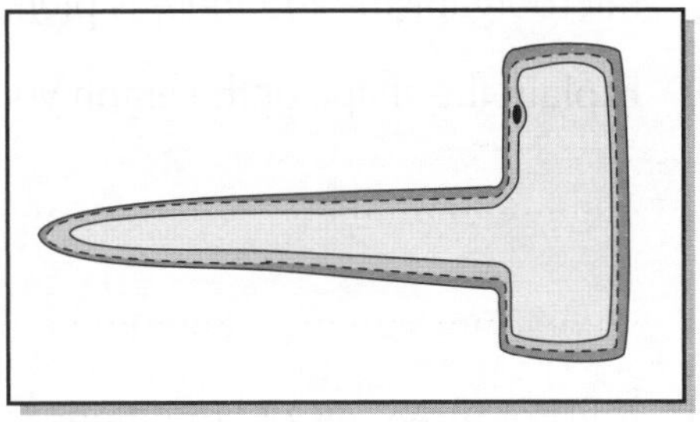

a) Name the type of cell shown.

....

b) What is the main **function** of this type of cell?

....

c) How is this type of cell adapted for its function?

....

d) Explain why minerals are **not** absorbed from the soil by **diffusion**.

....

e) Explain how these specialised cells absorb mineral ions from the soil.
Use the words **active transport**, **concentration**, **respiration** and **energy** in your answer.

....

....

Top Tip: Whenever you're talking about molecules moving into or out of cells, you need to stop and think. They could be moving by **osmosis**, **diffusion** or **active transport** — it all depends on what type of molecule they are and whether they're moving up or down the concentration gradient.

Module B4 — It's a Green World

Decay

Q1   Use the words provided to fill in the gaps in the paragraph below.

saprophytes   surface area   extracellular   detritivores   woodlice   detritus   rabbits

Saprophytes and detritivores are both types of decomposers. ....

include earthworms, maggots and .... They feed on dead and

decaying material known as .... As they do this, they increase the

.... of the material, which helps other decomposers to digest it.

....................................., for example fungi, also feed on dead material — but they

secrete digestive enzymes to break their food down by .... digestion.

Q2   Most decomposition is carried out by microorganisms. The **rate** of decay depends on three main things — **temperature**, **moisture** and **oxygen.**

a)   Sketch a line on the graph provided to show what you think will happen to the rate of decay as **temperature increases**. (Assume the temperature doesn't rise enough to damage the microorganisms and there is plenty of water and oxygen.)

b)   Explain the shape of the graph you have drawn.

....

....

c)   A list of **three** sets of conditions is shown in the box. **Rank** the sets of conditions from 1 to 3, 1 being the best for decay and 3 being the worst for decay.

Conditions	Rank
Dry, cold, no oxygen	....
Moist, warm, oxygen	....
Moist, cold, no oxygen	....

Q3   Draw lines to link the **food preservation methods** with how they reduce decay.

Canning   the acidic conditions kill any decomposers

Freezing   decomposers need water, so can't survive

Pickling   decomposers can't reproduce at such low temperatures

Drying   keeps decomposers out

Q4   Explain how storing tuna in **brine** (salt water) helps to preserve it.

....

Top Tip: It's easy to remember the methods we use to **stop** decomposers — as long as you know about the conditions microbes like for decay. So make darn well sure you've learnt them...

Intensive Farming

Q1 Match up each **intensive farming** method below with the correct description and advantage.

| using herbicides | kills insects | less energy wasted on movement and keeping warm |

| using insecticides | animals kept in small pens | more energy from the Sun is used by the crops |

| battery farming | kills weeds | less energy is transferred to another food chain |

Farmer Giles' methods were intense

Q2 **Plants** can be grown without soil.

a) What is the name of this technique?

....

b) What are the plants grown in?

....

c) Give an example of a plant that is often grown in this way.

....

d) Some of the things that need to be considered for this technique are listed below.
Tick to show whether each is an **advantage** or **disadvantage**.

Feature	Advantage	Disadvantage
i) No soil to anchor roots and support the plants.	☐	☐
ii) Lots of fertilisers need to be added.	☐	☐
iii) Diseases can be controlled more effectively.	☐	☐
iv) Mineral levels can be controlled more accurately.	☐	☐

Q3 Many people feel that **battery farming** animals is **unethical**.

a) Give one argument against battery farming.

....

b) Describe one other **ethical dilemma** that is raised by an aspect of intensive farming.

....

....

Pesticides and Biological Control

Q1 ▏Pesticides are chemicals that are used to kill pests.▕

Write down two problems that can be caused by the use of pesticides.

1. ....

2. ....

Q2 ▏Cockroaches were sprayed with a pesticide to control the size of their population.▕

Explain what effect this could have on the rest
of the food web shown.

....

....

....

cockroach   frog   fox

rabbit

Q3 ▏Biological control is an alternative to using pesticides.▕

a) What is biological control?

....

b) Write down two **advantages** and two **disadvantages** of using biological control.

Advantage 1: ....

Advantage 2: ....

Disadvantage 1: ....

Disadvantage 2: ....

Q4 ▏Pesticides that were being sprayed onto fields near to a
bird of prey's habitat were found in the birds in toxic levels.▕

*Birds of prey only
eat other animals.*

a) Suggest how the pesticide that was sprayed onto crops was found in the birds.

....

b) The amount of pesticide sprayed onto the field was carefully controlled to ensure it was at the
lowest concentration that would kill the pests. Suggest why the birds contained such large
amounts of the pesticide.

....

....

Alternatives to Intensive Farming

Q1 For each of the **intensive farming methods** below suggest an **organic farming alternative** and give one **advantage** of the alternative method.

a) **Using insecticides:** alternative method — ....

Advantage: ....

b) **Using herbicides:** alternative method — ....

Advantage: ....

c) **Using chemical fertilisers:** alternative method — ....

Advantage: ....

Q2 Describe the following organic farming methods and explain how they work.

a) Varying seed planting times

....

....

b) Crop rotation

....

....

....

Q3 Complete the following passage about **organic farming**, using the words from the list below.

wildlife	drawbacks	expensive	space	less	workers

Although organic farming methods have their obvious advantages, they also have several

.... Organic farming methods take up more ....

than their intensive alternatives, meaning that less land can be set aside for

.... and other uses. Organic farming requires more

.... (who all need to be paid), so organic produce is more

.... in the shops. Organic farming methods also produce much

.... food than can be produced using intensive farming techniques.

Mixed Questions — Module B4

Q1   Farmer MacDonald uses **chemical pesticides** on his crops.

a)   Explain why he uses these chemicals.

....

b)   What effect might the use of these pesticides have on the **buzzards** in the following food chain?

Apple tree → caterpillars → blackbirds → buzzards

....

....

c)   Some chemical pesticides are **persistent**. What does this mean?

....

d)   Farmer MacDonald also puts **fertiliser** on his crops. The fertiliser he uses
provides the crops with essential minerals to ensure healthy growth.

i) Which **two** minerals are most important for photosynthesis?

....

ii) Which mineral is vital for making proteins? ....

iii) Describe the symptoms of a plant with **potassium deficiency**.

....

....

Q2   The diagram below shows a cross section through a plant root.

a)   Draw arrows to link up each label to the correct part of the root.

phloem

root hair

xylem

b)   Complete the sentences below by circling the correct word(s) from each pair.

The concentration of minerals in the soil is **lower / higher** than in root hair cells. As a result,

minerals can't be absorbed by **diffusion / active transport** — instead they're absorbed by

diffusion / active transport. This requires energy from **photosynthesis / respiration** because

the minerals have to be moved against the concentration gradient.

Mixed Questions — Module B4

Q3   A student carried out a series of experiments on **osmosis**.

a)   Give a definition of the word 'osmosis'.

....

....

b)   In the first experiment potato chips were placed in different solutions. Their mass was recorded at the start and again after one day. The results are shown in the following table.

tube	start mass, g	end mass, g
A	1.20	1.45
B	1.40	1.21
C	1.32	1.32

Which tube (A, B or C) contained:

i) pure water?   ....

ii) dilute sugar solution?   ....

iii) concentrated sugar solution? ....

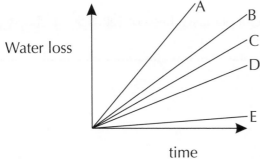
French Fries

c)   **i)**   In the second experiment **water** loss from a leafy shoot was measured. The shoot was exposed to **different conditions** and the water loss measured each time. The results are shown on the graph. Complete the table to show which line represents each set of conditions.

Water loss

A
B
C
D
E

time

Treatment	Line
kept in normal conditions	C
covered, clear plastic bag	
fanned, cool air	
fanned, warm air	
covered, black plastic bag	

ii) Explain the effect of **humidity** on transpiration rate.

....

....

....

Mixed Questions — Module B4

Q4 **Legumes** are plants that have nodules on their roots containing **nitrogen-fixing bacteria**.

a) Suggest why some farmers include legumes in their crop rotations.

....

b) Explain how and why an insufficient nitrogen intake affects a plant's development.

....

....

Q5 Seth investigated the effect of different concentrations of **carbon dioxide** on the rate of photosynthesis of his Swiss cheese plant. The results are shown on the graph below.

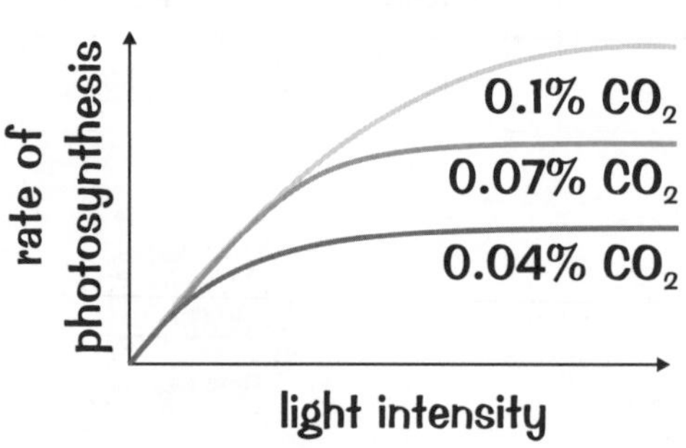

a) Describe how increasing the concentration of CO_2 affects the rate of photosynthesis.

....

....

b) Name one other factor that would affect the rate of photosynthesis of Seth's Swiss cheese plant.

....

c) Explain why the graph levels off eventually.

....

....

d) Give three features of leaves that make them well adapted to the **diffusion** of carbon dioxide.

1. ....

2. ....

3. ....

The History of the Atom

Q1 The theory of **atomic structure** has changed a lot over the past two hundred years. Draw lines to place these landmark theories on the time line in the **correct order**.

beginning of the 19th century

present day

| J J Thomson's plum pudding model. | Bohr's electron shell theory. | Dalton's solid spheres. | Rutherford's theory of the nuclear atom. |

Q2 **Bohr's** theory was pretty close to our present day view of the atom.

a) Describe Bohr's model of the atom.

....

....

b) Bohr's model was different to previous theories. Why was his theory accepted by scientists?

....

Q3 J J Thomson developed the **plum pudding model** of the atom.

a) Draw and label a diagram of this model in the box on the right.

Remember to label the positive and negative parts.

b) Describe how J J Thompson's model of the atom differed from Dalton's model of the atom.

....

....

....

Q4 Geiger and Marsden conducted an experiment known as the '**gold foil experiment**'.

a) Briefly describe how this experiment was conducted.

....

b) Describe what they observed.

....

c) Explain why these results were significant.

....

....

Atoms

Q1   **Complete** the following sentences.

a)   Neutral atoms have a charge of ....

b)   The nucleus is made up of .... and ....

c)   Atoms have a mass of about .... grams.

d)   A neutral atom has the same number of .... and ....

e)   Atoms have a radius of about .... metres.

Q2   **Complete** this table.

Particle	Mass	Charge
Proton	1	
	1	0
Electron		−1

Q3   Elements have a **mass number** and an **atomic number**.

a)   What does the **mass number** of an element tell you?

   ....

b)   What does the **atomic number** of an element tell you?

   ....

c)   Fill in this table using a periodic table.

Element	Symbol	Mass Number	Number of Protons	Number of Electrons	Number of Neutrons
Sodium	Na		11		
		16	8	8	8
Neon			10	10	10
	Ca			20	20

Q4   In the periodic table **carbon** (C) is written like this: $^{12}_{6}\text{C}$

a)   Circle the mass number.

b)   Underline the atomic number.

c)   How many protons does carbon have?   ....

d)   How many electrons does this carbon have?   ....

e)   How many neutrons does this carbon have?   ....

Elements and Isotopes

Q1 Select from these **elements** to answer the following questions.

iodine   nickel   silicon   sodium   radon   krypton   calcium

a) Which two elements are in the same group? .... and ....

b) Name two elements which are in Period 3. .... and ....

c) Name an element in Group 1. ....

d) Name an element with seven electrons in its outer shell. ....

e) Name a non-metal which is not in Group 8. ....

You can use the periodic table to help you for this one.

Q2 Tick the correct boxes to show whether these statements are **true** or **false**.   **True False**

a) Elements in the same **group** have the same number of electrons in their outer shell. ☐ ☐

b) The periodic table shows the elements in order of ascending **atomic mass**. ☐ ☐

c) Each **column** in the periodic table contains elements with similar properties. ☐ ☐

d) The periodic table is made up of all the known compounds. ☐ ☐

e) There are more than 100 known elements. ☐ ☐

f) Each new period in the periodic table represents another full shell of electrons. ☐ ☐

g) Elements in Group 6 have a full outer shell of electrons. ☐ ☐

Q3 Choose the correct words to **complete** this paragraph.

element	isotopes	protons	neutrons

.... are different atomic forms of the same .... which have the

same number of .... but a different number of ....

Q4 Which of the following atoms are **isotopes** of each other? Explain your answer.

W $^{12}_{6}C$ X $^{4}_{2}He$ Y $^{14}_{6}C$ Z $^{14}_{7}N$

Answer: .... and ....

Explanation: ....

Module C4 — The Periodic Table

History of the Periodic Table

Q1 Which of the following statements about **Mendeleev's** Table of Elements are **true** and which are **false**? Tick the correct boxes.

	True	False

a) Mendeleev arranged the elements in order of increasing atomic number. ☐ ☐

b) Mendeleev was able to predict the properties of undiscovered elements. ☐ ☐

c) Elements with similar properties appeared in the same rows. ☐ ☐

Q2 Describe how **Döbereiner** chose elements for his **triads**.

....

....

Q3 When **Newlands** arranged the known elements in order of **atomic mass** in 1864, the first three rows were as shown.

	1					**2**
H	Li	Be	B	C	N	O
F	Na	Mg	Al	Si	P	S
Cl	K	Ca	Cr	Ti	Mn	Fe

a) In which of the two highlighted groups do the elements have similar properties?   ....

b) This arrangement of elements was known as 'Newlands' Octaves'. Why did Newlands arrange the elements in rows of seven?

....

c) Give one criticism of Newlands' arrangement of the elements.

....

Q4 Mendeleev left **gaps** in his Table of Elements to keep elements with similar properties in the same groups. He predicted that elements would eventually be discovered to fill the gaps. For example, he predicted the discovery of an element that would fill a gap in his Group 4 and called it '**ekasilicon**'.

Element	Density g/cm³
carbon	2.27
silicon	2.33
'ekasilicon'	
tin	7.29
lead	11.34

The table shows the **densities** of known elements in this group.

a) 'Ekasilicon' was eventually discovered and given another name. Use the information in the table to decide which of the elements below is 'ekasilicon'. Circle your choice.

palladium, 12.02 g/cm³   germanium, 5.32 g/cm³   beryllium, 1.85 g/cm³   copper, 8.93 g/cm³

b) Describe two other pieces of evidence that have supported Mendeleev's arrangement of the elements.

1. ....

....

2. ....

....

Electron Shells

Q1 a) Tick the boxes to show whether the statements are **true** or **false**.

True False

   i) Electrons occupy shells. ☐ ☐

   ii) The highest energy levels are always filled first. ☐ ☐

   iii) The first shell can hold 8 electrons. ☐ ☐

   iv) Noble gases have a full outer shell of electrons. ☐ ☐

   v) The third shell can hold 8 electrons. ☐ ☐

b) Write out corrected versions of the **false** statements.

....

....

....

Q2 Identify **two** things that are wrong with this diagram.

1...

....

2...

....

Use the periodic table to help you here.

Q3 Write out the **electronic configuration** for each of the following elements.

a) Beryllium ....

b) Oxygen ....

c) Silicon ....

d) Calcium ....

e) Aluminium ....

f) Argon ....

Q4 Write down the **period** and **group** for elements with the following electronic structures.

a) **2, 8, 4** period ....

   group ....

b) **2, 2** period ....

   group ....

c) **2, 3** period ....

   group ....

d) **2, 8, 8** period ....

   group ....

Electron Shells

Q5   **Chlorine** has an atomic number of 17.

a)   What is chlorine's electron configuration? ....

b)   Draw the electrons on the shells in the diagram.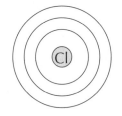

Q6   Draw the **full electronic structures** of these elements.
(The first three have been done for you.)

Hydrogen

Helium

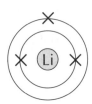

Lithium

a)   Carbon

b) Nitrogen

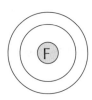

c)   Fluorine

d)   Sodium

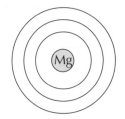

e) Magnesium

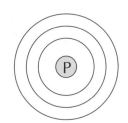

f)   Phosphorus

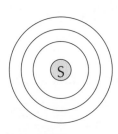

g)   Sulfur

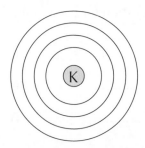

h)   Potassium

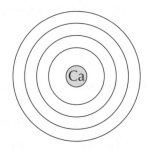

i)   Calcium

Q7   Use a periodic table to identify these elements from their electronic configuration.

a)   2, 8, 8, 1   ....

b)   2, 8, 4   ....

Top Tips: Once you've learnt the 'electron shell rules' these are pretty easy — the first shell can only take 2 electrons, and the second and third shells a maximum of 8 each. Don't forget them.

Ionic Bonding

Q1 Fill in the gaps in the sentences below by choosing the correct words from the box.

protons	charged particles	repelled by
electrons	ions	attracted to	neutral particles

a) In ionic bonding atoms lose or gain .... to form ....

b) Ions are ....

c) Ions with opposite charges are strongly .... each other.

Q2 **Magnesium oxide** is formed from two ions.

a) What name is given to the structure of magnesium oxide?

....

b) Circle the correct words to explain why magnesium oxide has a high melting point.

> Magnesium oxide has very **strong** / **weak** attraction between the **negative** / **positive** magnesium ions and the **negative** / **positive** oxygen ions. This means that it takes a **small** / **large** amount of energy to overcome the attraction and melt the compound.

c) Sodium chloride is another ionic compound. Sodium forms 1^+ ions and chlorine forms 1^- ions.

   i) Will sodium chloride have a higher or lower melting point than magnesium chloride? ....

   ii) Explain your answer.

....

....

....

....

Q3 Mike conducts an experiment to find out if **sodium chloride** conducts electricity. He tests the compound when it's solid, when it's dissolved in water and when it's molten.

	Conducts electricity?
When solid	
When dissolved in water	
When molten	

a) Complete the table of results opposite.

b) Explain your answers to part a).

....

....

Ions and Ionic Compounds

Q1 Tick the correct boxes to show whether the following statements are **true** or **false**.

True False

a) Ions of metals and non-metals attract one another to form ionic compounds. ☐ ☐

b) Metals form negatively charged ions. ☐ ☐

c) Ions with a 2+ charge have gained 2 electrons. ☐ ☐

d) Elements in Group 7 gain electrons when they react. ☐ ☐

e) Atoms form ions because they are more stable when they have full outer shells. ☐ ☐

f) Elements with a full outer shell are very reactive. ☐ ☐

g) The number of electrons lost or gained is equal to the charge on the ion. ☐ ☐

Q2 Here are some elements and the ions they form:

beryllium, Be^{2+} potassium, K^+ iodine, I^- sulfur, S^{2-}

Make sure the charges on the ions balance.

Write down the formulas of four compounds which can be made using these elements.

1. ....   2. ....

3. ....   4. ....

Q3 Draw '**dot and cross**' diagrams showing the formation of the following ionic compounds:

a) sodium oxide (Na_2O)

b) magnesium chloride ($MgCl_2$)

c) magnesium oxide (MgO)

Top Tips: The big thing to remember about ionic compounds is... the charges always **balance**. The oppositely charged ions then strongly attract each other to create an ionic compound. Lovely.

Module C4 — The Periodic Table

Covalent Bonding

Q1 Indicate whether each statement is **true** or **false**.

True False

a) Covalent bonding involves sharing electron pairs. ☐ ☐

b) Metals form covalent bonds. ☐ ☐

c) Some atoms can make both ionic and covalent bonds. ☐ ☐

d) Hydrogen can form two covalent bonds. ☐ ☐

e) Carbon can form four covalent bonds. ☐ ☐

"Oi, give me that electron big nose!"

Q2 Carbon dioxide and water are both covalently bonded molecules.
Complete these sentences by circling the correct word from each pair.

a) Substances that contain covalent bonds usually have **giant** / **simple** molecular structures.

b) Atoms within covalent molecules are held together by **strong** / **weak** covalent bonds.

c) Intermolecular forces between water molecules are **strong** / **weak**.
This results in **high** / **low** melting and boiling points.

d) Carbon dioxide has no free electrons so it **does** / **doesn't** conduct electricity.

Q3 Complete the following diagrams by adding **electrons**. Only the **outer shells** are shown.

Use • and x to show the electrons from the different elements.

a) Hydrogen
(H_2)

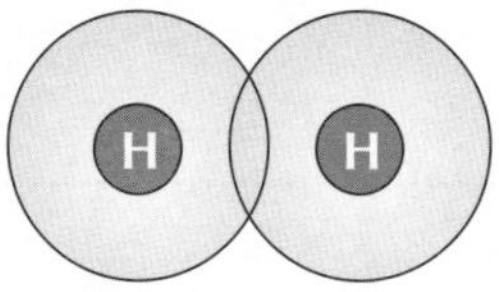

H   H

d) Water (H_2O)

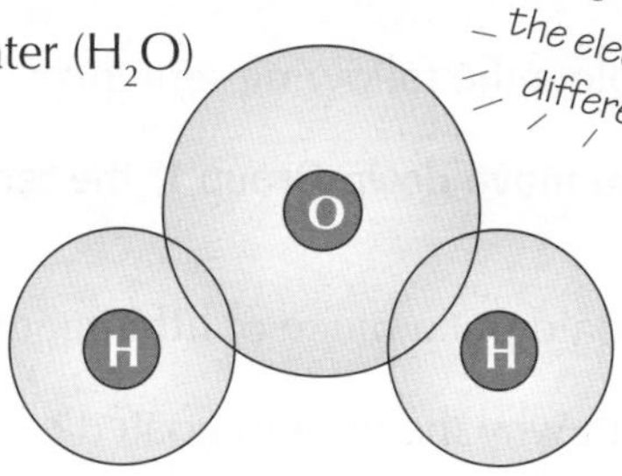

O
H   H

b) Chlorine
(Cl_2)

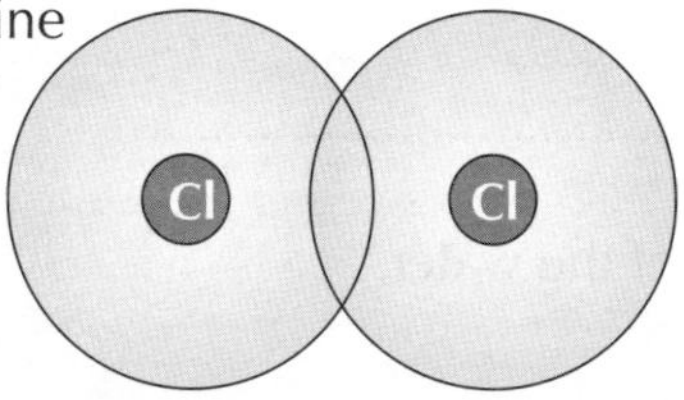

Cl   Cl

e) Methane
(CH_4)

H
H   C   H
H

c) Carbon dioxide
(CO_2)

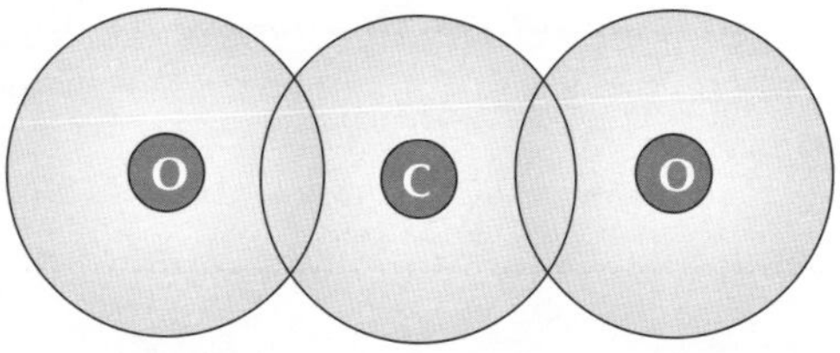

O   C   O

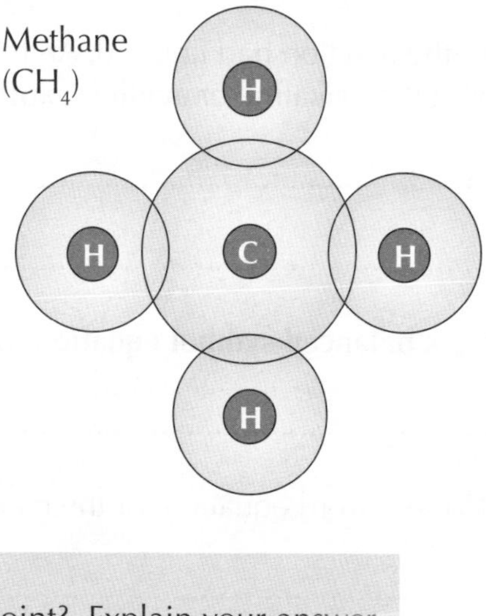

Q4 Chlorine (Cl_2) has a simple molecular structure.
Do you think that it will have a high or low boiling point? Explain your answer.

....

....

Group 1 — Alkali Metals

Q1 Indicate whether the statements below are **true** or **false**.

		True	False
a)	Alkali metals readily gain electrons to form 1^+ ions.	☐	☐
b)	Alkali metals form covalent compounds by sharing electrons.	☐	☐
c)	Alkali metals are stored in oil to stop them reacting with oxygen and water in the air.	☐	☐
d)	Alkali metal atoms all have a single electron in their outer shell.	☐	☐
e)	Alkali metals are hard.	☐	☐
f)	Alkali metals have similar properties because they all react to lose one electron.	☐	☐

Q2 The table shows the **melting points** of some Group 1 metals.

Element	Melting point (°C)
Li	181
Na	98
K	63
Rb	39
Cs	?

a) What is unusual about the **melting points** of the alkali metals compared to other metals?

....

b) Would you expect the melting point of **caesium** to be higher or lower than **rubidium**? Explain your answer.

....

c) Complete the following sentence:

As you move down Group 1, the reactivity of the atoms ....

Q3 Archibald put a piece of **lithium** into a beaker of water.

a) Explain why the lithium floated on top of the water.

....

b) After the reaction had finished, Archibald tested the pH of the water. Would it be **alkaline** or **acidic**? Explain your answer.

....

....

c) Write a **balanced symbol equation** for the reaction.

....

d) i) Write a word equation for the reaction between rubidium and water.

....

ii) Would you expect the reaction between rubidium and water to be **more** or **less** vigorous than the reaction between lithium and water? Explain your answer.

....

"squeaky pop!"

Group 1 — Alkali Metals

Q4 Alkali metal compounds emit characteristic **colours** when put in a flame.

a) Selina has three powdered samples of alkali metal compounds. Describe an experiment she could carry out to help her identify the alkali metal present.

....

....

....

....

b) Which **alkali metal** is present in:

i) an alkali metal nitrate (found in gunpowder) that produces a lilac flame? ....

ii) a street lamp that emits an orange light? ....

iii) fireworks that produce red flames? ....

Q5 Sodium and potassium are **alkali metals**.

a) Draw the electronic arrangements of a **sodium atom** and a **potassium atom** in the space provided.

b) **i)** Write a balanced symbol equation to show the formation of a sodium ion from a sodium atom.

....

ii) Is this process oxidation or reduction? Explain your answer.

....

c) Why do sodium and potassium have similar properties?

....

d) Why is potassium more reactive than sodium?

....

....

Top Tips: All the alkali metals have a single outer electron, which they're dead keen to get rid of so they have a nice full outer shell. As you move down the group the outer electron gets further away from the nucleus so it's lost more easily — this makes the elements more reactive as you go down the group.

Group 7 — Halogens

Q1 Draw lines to match each halogen to its **description**.

chlorine (Cl$_2$)

iodine (I$_2$)

bromine (Br$_2$)

dense green gas

orange liquid

dark grey solid

Hubba hubba

Q2 Tick the correct boxes to say whether these statements are **true** or **false**.

		True	False
a)	Chlorine gas is made up of molecules which each contain three chlorine atoms.	☐	☐
b)	The halogens become less reactive as you go down the group.	☐	☐
c)	Chlorine and bromine are poisonous.	☐	☐
d)	The halogens readily gain electrons to form 1$^+$ ions.	☐	☐

Q3 Chlorine and bromine are both **halogens**.

a) Draw the electron arrangements of a **chlorine atom** and a **chloride ion** in the space provided.

b) i) Write a balanced symbol equation to show the formation of chloride ions from a chlorine molecule.

....

ii) Is this process oxidation or reduction? Explain your answer.

....

c) Why do chlorine and bromine have similar properties?

....

d) Why is bromine less reactive than chlorine?

....

....

Group 7 — Halogens

Q4 **Sodium** was reacted with **bromine vapour** using the equipment shown. White crystals of a new solid were formed during the reaction.

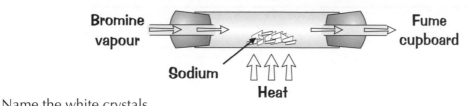

Bromine vapour

Sodium

Heat

Fume cupboard

a) Name the white crystals.

....

b) Write a balanced symbol equation for the reaction.

....

c) Would you expect the above reaction to be faster or slower than a similar reaction between:

i) sodium and iodine vapour? Explain your answer.

....

ii) sodium and chlorine vapour? Explain your answer.

....

Q5 Equal volumes of **bromine solution** were added to two test tubes, each containing a different **potassium halide solution**. The results are shown in the table.

SOLUTION	RESULT
potassium chloride	no colour change
potassium iodide	colour change

a) Explain these results.

....

....

....

b) Write a **balanced symbol equation** for the reaction in the potassium iodide solution.

....

c) Would you expect a reaction between:

i) bromine solution and potassium astatide? ....

ii) bromine solution and potassium fluoride? ....

Metals

Q1   Draw a diagram in the space below to show the arrangement of the particles in a typical **metal**. Label the **ions** and the **free electrons**, and show any relevant charges.

An irrelevant charge.

Q2   The table shows the properties of **four elements** found in the periodic table.

ELEMENT	MELTING POINT (°C)	DENSITY (g/cm³)	ELECTRICAL CONDUCTIVITY
A	1084	8.9	Excellent
B	–39	13.6	Very good
C	3500	3.51	Very poor
D	1536	7.87	Very good

a)   Which three of the above elements are most likely to be **metals**?

....

b)   Explain how you know the other element is **not** a metal.

....

....

Q3   Circle the phrase which best describes **metallic bonding**.

Strong attraction between delocalised electrons and close packed positive metal ions.

Strong attraction between bonding electrons and close packed positive metal ions.

Strong attraction between delocalised electrons and close packed negative metal ions.

Q4   Explain how **electricity** is conducted through metals.

....

....

Metals

Q5 Complete the following sentences by choosing from the words in the box.

Don't use any words more than once.

hammered	weak	low	high	strong	malleable	folded

a) Metals have a .... tensile strength.

b) Metals are .... and hard to break.

c) Metals can be .... into different shapes because they are ....

Q6 Explain why most metals have **high melting points**.

....

....

Q7 **Metals** are used for different things depending on their **properties**.

For each of the uses below, choose the most suitable metal from the list and state one property of the metal that makes it suitable for this purpose.

stainless steel   **copper**   **aluminium**   **steel**

a) Structures like bridges.

    Metal ....

    Property ....

b) Aeroplanes.

    Metal ....

    Property ....

c) Cutlery.

    Metal ....

    Property ....

d) Electrical wiring.

    Metal ....

    Property ....

Top Tips: Okay, so metals form weird bonds. How come the electrons can go wandering about like that? Well actually, that's just the kind of question you **don't** need to ask yourself right now. Don't stress about it, just learn the key phrases examiners like — **'sea of delocalised electrons,'** etc.

Module C4 — The Periodic Table

Superconductors and Transition Metals

Q1   Draw lines to match the transition metal to the process it catalyses.

iron   hydrogenation of alkenes

nickel   ammonia production

Q2   Complete the passage below by circling the correct word(s) from each pair.

> Most metals are in the transition block found **at the left / in the middle** of the
>
> periodic table. They are generally **good / poor** conductors of heat and electricity,
>
> have high **densities / volatility** and **low / high** melting points. Their compounds are
>
> **colourful / shiny** and, like the metals themselves, are often effective **fuels / catalysts**.

Q3   Under normal conditions **all** metals have **electrical resistance**.

a)   Describe how electrical resistance causes energy to be wasted.

....

....

b)   What is a superconductor? ....

c)   Give three possible uses of superconducting wires.

1. ....

2. ....

3. ....

d)   Explain a drawback of using today's superconductors.

....

....

Q4   'Colourful chemical gardens' can be made by sprinkling
transition metal salts into **sodium silicate solution**.
Transition metal silicate crystals grow upwards as shown.

sodium silicate
solution

transition
metal silicates

a)   Why do you think transition metal salts are used?

....

b)   Suggest three colours that you would be likely to see in the garden if iron(II) sulfate,
iron(III) chloride and copper(II) sulfate salts are used.

....

Thermal Decomposition and Precipitation

Q1 Draw lines to match the type of reaction with its description.

thermal decomposition

when a substance breaks down into two or more simpler substances when heated

precipitation

where two solutions react and an insoluble solid is formed

Q2 Neil heats some **green** copper carbonate, $CuCO_3$. He is left with a **black** solid.

a) How can Neil tell that a reaction has taken place?

....

b) What type of reaction has taken place? ....

c) Write a word equation for this reaction.

....

d) Describe how you could **test** for **carbon dioxide**.

....

....

Q3 Write **balanced symbol equations** for the thermal decomposition of the following substances.

a) zinc carbonate, $ZnCO_3$

....

b) iron(II) carbonate, $FeCO_3$

....

c) copper(II) carbonate, $CuCO_3$

....

d) manganese(II) carbonate, $MnCO_3$

....

Top Tips: Thermal decomposition — what a name. But it's not as difficult as it sounds. Take one reactant. Heat it up until it falls apart into two or more bits and there you go — one thermal decomposition reaction. Simple. The tricky bit is learning all those symbol equations...

Thermal Decomposition and Precipitation

Q4   Clear, blue **copper(II) sulfate solution** and clear, colourless **sodium hydroxide** solution were mixed. The liquid went cloudy and pale blue. After a while a **pale blue solid** was left at the bottom and the liquid was **clear** again.

a) What type of reaction has occurred? ....

b) Name the blue solid formed.

....

c) Write a balanced symbol equation for this reaction.

....

d) Write a symbol equation to show the formation of the pale blue solid.

....

Q5   Cilla adds a few drops of **NaOH** solution to solutions of different **metal compounds**.

a) Complete her table of results.

Compound	Metal Ion	Colour of Precipitate
copper(II) sulfate		blue
iron(II) sulfate		
iron(III) chloride	Fe^{3+}	
copper(II) chloride		

b) Write a balanced symbol equation for the reaction of copper(II) chloride with sodium hydroxide.

....

c) Complete the balanced ionic equation for the reaction of iron(II) ions with hydroxide ions.

These reactions could also happen with lithium hydroxide (LiOH) or potassium hydroxide (KOH).

Fe^{2+} + ... OH^- → ....

d) Write a balanced ionic equation for the reaction of **iron(III) ions** with hydroxide ions.

....

e) Explain how this type of reaction could be used to help identify unknown metal ions.

....

....

....

Water Purity

Q1   There are a variety of water resources in the UK.

a)   Which one of the following water resources is a source of 'groundwater'? Circle your answer.

reservoirs   aquifers   rivers   lakes

b)   Name three important uses of water in **industrial processes**.

....

....

Q2   Explain why it is important to conserve water.

....

....

Q3   Water is **treated** before it reaches our homes.

a)   Number the stages 1– 4 to show the correct order of the processes in a **water treatment** plant.

☐ Sedimentation   ☐ Filtration through sand beds

☐ Chlorination   ☐ Filtration through a wire mesh

b)   Why are two filtration processes needed? ....

....

c)   Name a chemical used in the sedimentation process. ....

d)   Why are the purification processes unable to remove impurities such as ammonium nitrate?

....

e)   Why is chlorination used in the purification process?

....

Q4   Helen's house has an **old plumbing system**. She's concerned about **pollutants** in the tap water.

a)   What form of pollution in the tap water could be caused by the plumbing system?

....

b)   Helen's water supply comes from a reservoir located in an area of intensive agriculture.
Suggest **two** other forms of pollutant which could be present in the tap water.

....

Q5   Some countries get fresh water by **distilling** sea water. Give **one** disadvantage of using this method.

....

Module C4 — The Periodic Table

Testing Water Purity

Q1 Sodium sulfate reacts with **barium chloride** in a precipitation reaction.

a) What is a **precipitation reaction**?

....

b) Complete the word equation for this reaction.

sodium sulfate + barium chloride → barium .... + ...

c) Complete and balance the symbol equation for this reaction.

Na_2SO_4 + ... → .... + ... NaCl

HINT: The sulfate ion is SO_4^{2-} and the barium ion is Ba^{2+}.

d) State the **colour** of the precipitate formed in this reaction.

....

Q2 Sam creates a flow chart as a key to help her identify **halide anions** present in a sample of water.

a) Finish the flow chart by completing the empty boxes.

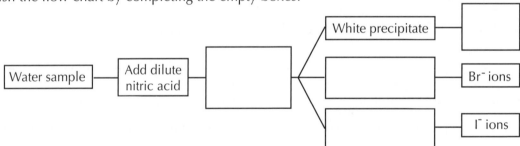

b) Complete the following balanced symbol equations involved in testing for halide ions.

i) $AgNO_3$ + KCl → .... + KNO_3

ii) .... + ... → AgI + $NaNO_3$

iii) Ag^+ + Br^- → ....

Remember you have to have the same number of atoms on each side of the equation.

Q3 Jukka tests his local duck pond for pollutants using aqueous $AgNO_3$ and $BaCl_2$ solutions. After testing a sample of the water with each of the solutions a **white precipitate** is formed.

State the **two** ions that could be present in the solution.

1. ....

2. ....

Mixed Questions — Module C4

Q1   Hydrogen atoms can exist as three **isotopes** — ^{1}**H** (hydrogen), ^{2}**H** (deuterium) and ^{3}**H** (tritium).

a) What is an isotope?

....

b) Complete the table.

isotope	number of protons	number of neutrons	number of electrons
^{1}H			
^{2}H			
^{3}H			

c) The atomic number is often left out of the isotope symbol.
For instance, it is acceptable to write ^{12}**C** for carbon-12 rather than $^{12}_{6}$**C**.

i) Define the term **atomic number**.

....

ii) Explain why the atomic number can be left out of the isotope symbol.

....

Q2   **Lithium** is a metallic element in **Group 1** of the periodic table.

a) Draw a diagram to show the electronic
structure of a lithium atom.

Use the periodic table to help you.

b) Explain how lithium ions usually form.

....

c) **Fluorine** is in **Group 7** of the periodic table. Its electronic structure is shown below.

i) Draw a diagram to show the electronic
structure of a fluoride **ion**.

ii) Give the chemical formula
for the compound that forms
between lithium and fluorine.

....

d) Complete this table.

Ion	Symbol	Mass Number	Number of Protons	Number of Electrons	Number of Neutrons
Lithium		7			
Fluorine			9		10

Mixed Questions — Module C4

Q3   The table below gives some data for five **elements**.

Element	Melting point (°C)	Density (g/cm³)	Conducts electricity as solid?	Oxide of element	
				Colour (at 20 °C)	State (at 20 °C)
A	1455	8.9	Yes	Green	Solid
B	44	1.82	No	White	Solid
C	3550	3.51	No	Colourless	Gas
D	1535	7.86	Yes	Red	Solid
E	98	0.97	Yes	White	Solid

a)   Two of the elements are transition elements. Identify them and explain your answers.

....

....

b)   Give a use for one named transition element.

Transition element: ....   Use: ....

Q4   Scientists are trying to develop superconductors that work at **higher temperatures** than is currently possible.

a)   What temperature would it be ideal for superconductors to work at?

....

b)   A scientist has developed a high temperature superconductor.
Explain why he/she would tell other scientists about the discovery.

....

....

Q5   Ronald has been given a mystery test tube containing solution X. He tests the solution using different chemicals. His results are shown below.

a)   Identify solution X.

....

b)   Explain your answer to part **a)**.

....

....

Test	Result
$AgNO_3$	Nothing happened
$BaCl_2$	A white precipitate was formed
NaOH	A pale blue precipitate was formed

....

Mixed Questions — Module C4

Q6 The diagram shows the apparatus used to react **chlorine** with **magnesium**.

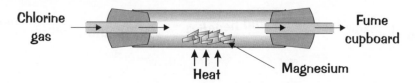

a) Why is it not possible to use the same apparatus to react iodine with magnesium?

....

b) Complete the chemical equation for the reaction: $Mg + Cl_2 \rightarrow$ ....

c) What type of bonding is present in the product? ....

d) Draw a dot and cross diagram to show the formation of magnesium chloride from magnesium and chlorine atoms.

e) Solid magnesium chloride does not conduct electricity. However, when magnesium chloride is dissolved in water or is molten it does conduct electricity. Explain these facts.

....

....

Q7 Metals are good **electrical conductors**. Explain why, using ideas about structure and bonding.

....

....

....

Q8 Iodine has a **simple molecular structure**.

a) What type of bonding binds the iodine atoms together in each molecule? ....

b) Explain why iodine has a low melting point.

....

....

c) Predict whether iodine is likely to be able to conduct electricity. Justify your prediction.

....

....

Static Electricity

Q1   **Circle** the pairs of charges that would attract each other and **underline** those that would repel.

positive and positive   positive and negative   negative and positive   negative and negative

Q2   Fill in the **gaps** in these sentences with the words below.

electrons	positive	static	insulating	negative

.... electricity can build up when two .... materials

are rubbed together. The .... move from one material onto the other.

This leaves a .... charge on one of the materials and a

.... charge on the other.

Q3   The sentences below are wrong. Write out a **correct** version for each.

> Polythene is an insulating material.

a)   An insulating rod becomes negatively charged when
rubbed with a duster because it loses electrons. .

....

....

b)   A charged polythene rod will repel small pieces of paper if they are placed near it.

....

....

c)   The closer two charged objects are together, the less strongly they attract or repel.

....

....

d)   If a positively charged object is connected to earth by a metal strap,
electrons flow through the strap from the object to the ground.

....

....

e)   Build-up of static can cause sparks if the distance between the object and the earth is big enough.

....

....

More on Static Electricity

Q1 Tick the boxes to show whether the following statements are **true** or **false**.

	True	False
a) Electrons are negatively charged particles.	☐	☐
b) Areas of positive charge are caused by the movement of positive charges.	☐	☐
c) Negatively charged areas occur because electrons are attracted to each other.	☐	☐

Q2 A library had to be closed after **nylon** carpets were fitted. People complained of **electric shocks** when they touched the **metal** handrail on the stairs. Explain why they were experiencing shocks.

....

....

Q3 Choose from the words below to complete the passage.

fuel   explosion   metal   paper rollers   wood   grain chutes   sparks   earthing   plastic

> Static electricity can be dangerous when refuelling cars. If too much static builds up, there
>
> might be .... which could set fire to the ....
>
> This could lead to an .... To prevent this happening, the nozzle is
>
> made of .... so the charge is conducted away. There are similar safety
>
> problems with .... and ....

Q4 Three friends are talking about some of the effects of **static electricity**.

Why does my hair sometimes stick out and cling to the brush? — Lisa

Why is the TV screen always dusty — my mum cleans it all the time? — Sara

Why do I hear a crackling sound when I take off my jumper? — Tim

Answer their questions in terms of the **attraction** and **repulsion** between charges.

Lisa: ....

....

Sara: ....

....

Tim: ....

....

Uses of Static Electricity

Q1 The diagram shows an **electrostatic** paint sprayer.

a) How do the drops of paint become **charged**?

....

b) Why does this help produce a **fine spray**?

....

c) Explain how the paint drops are **attracted** to the object being sprayed.

....

d) Explain why the object being painted doesn't need to be **turned** round while it is being sprayed.

....

Q2 Complete this paragraph by choosing words from the list below.

precipitator	negative	plates	charge	particles	positive
heavy	attracted	fall off	electron	compressed	

Smoke contains tiny .... The smoke can be cleaned up with a dust

.... One sort uses a wire grid with a high negative .... to

give the particles a negative charge. They then pass between two metal ....

which have a .... charge. The particles are .... to

the plates. The particles clump together and when they are .... enough,

they ....

Q3 A **defibrillator** is a machine used by emergency medical staff to give **electric shocks**.

a) What are defibrillators used for?

....

b) How is the electricity **transferred** to the patient?

....

c) Explain what **safety** precautions are taken when using a defibrillator and why.

....

....

<u>Charge in Circuits</u>

Q1 Use the words below to complete the passage.
You may need to use some words **more than once**.

protons	electrons	resistance	voltage	increase	reduce

Current is the flow of .... around a circuit. Current flows through

a component which has a .... across it. Resistance tends to

.... the flow. To increase the current in a circuit you can

.... the resistance or .... the voltage.

Q2 Draw lines to connect the **quantities** with their **units** and unit **symbols**.

Current   volts

Resistance   amps

Voltage   ohms

Q3 A **current** flows around an electrical circuit.

a) If the circuit is **broken**, what happens to the current?

....

b) Give an example of a safety feature designed to break a circuit.

....

Q4 The flow of **electricity in circuits** can be compared to the flow of **water in pipes**.

a) In a water 'circuit', what is equivalent to electrical **current**?

....

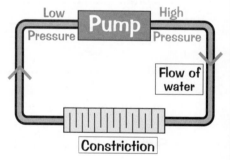

b) If there is a **water pump** in the system,
what electrical device does it correspond to?

....

c) What corresponds to electrical **resistance** in a water 'circuit'?

....

d) The pump is turned up. What would the equivalent action be in an electrical circuit?

....

Top Tips: The current is the flow of electrons, which are pushed around a circuit by the
voltage. The greater the voltage, the more current flows. Anything that slows the flow of electrons
down is a resistor. Slowing the electrons decreases the current. Make sure you get the hang of this
and you'll be scooping up the marks like a small child let loose at the pick and mix counter. Enjoy.

Plugs and Fuses

Q1   Describe the main difference between a **fuse** and a **circuit breaker**.

....

....

Q2   Put these events in the **correct order** to describe what happens when
a **fault** occurs in an earthed kettle. Label the events from 1 to 4.

☐ **The device is isolated from the live wire.**   ☐ **A big current flows out through the earth wire.**

☐ **A big surge in current blows the fuse.**   ☐ **A fault allows the live wire
to touch the metal case.**

Q3   Tom is making **toast** and **tea** for breakfast. His house has a **230 V** mains electricity supply.

a)   Tom's toaster draws **4 A** of current. Calculate the power rating of his toaster.

....

b)   Tom puts on the kettle to make tea. The kettle has a power rating of **1725 W**.
How much current does the kettle draw?

....

Q4   Explain the function of each of the wires found in a **plug**.

Neutral: ....

....

Live: ....

....

Earth: ....

....

～～～	= Neutral
━━	= Live
∿∿∿∿	= Earth

Insulating materials don't
conduct electricity.

Q5   A '**double insulated**' hairdryer uses a current of **3.7 A**.

a)   Andrea has fuses rated 3 A, 5 A and 13 A.
Which fuse should she fit in the plug for the hairdryer? ....

b)   Why does the hairdryer **not** need an **earth wire**?

....

Resistance

Q1 Complete these sentences by **circling** the correct word from each pair.

a) Increasing the voltage **increases** / **decreases** the current that flows.

b) If the voltage is constant, to increase the current you need to **increase** / **decrease** the resistance.

c) If the resistance is increased, **more** / **less** current will flow if the voltage is constant.

Q2 Tick the boxes to show whether these statements are **true** or **false**.

	True	False
A variable resistor is used to alter the current passing through a circuit.	☐	☐
Longer wires have more resistance than shorter wires.	☐	☐
Thinner wires have less resistance than thicker wires.	☐	☐

Q3 Fill in the **missing values** in the table below.

Ir-resistor-ble.

Voltage (V)	Current (A)	Resistance (Ω)
6	2	
8		2
	3	3
4	8	
2		4
	0.5	2

Q4 Fabio sets up a standard circuit using a **variable resistor** to test the resistance of a material.

a) **Label** the standard test circuit components using the words in the box below.

voltmeter	material
variable resistor	ammeter

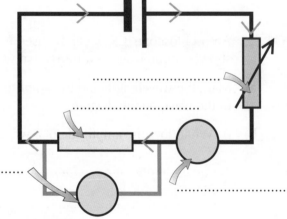

b) Fabio sets the variable resistor at **zero** resistance. He measures a current of **2.4 A** and a voltage of **6 V**. Calculate the resistance of the material.

....

c) How would Fabio use the variable resistor to help get a **reliable** result from his experiment?

....

....

Ultrasound Treatments and Scans

Q1 Indicate whether the following statements are **true** or **false**.

True False

Ultrasound waves have frequencies greater than 20 000 Hz. ☐ ☐

X-rays are used for prenatal scanning. ☐ ☐

Ultrasound can cause cancer if a patient is exposed to a high dose. ☐ ☐

X-rays travel easily through soft tissue. ☐ ☐

Ultrasound and X-rays are both good ways of looking at broken bones in the body. ☐ ☐

Q2 Sound waves are **longitudinal** waves.

a) Describe the difference between **longitudinal** and **transverse** waves.

....

....

b) What is meant by the **frequency** of a wave?

....

c) When sound waves travel through a material they produce **compressions** and **rarefactions**. What do these words mean?

....

....

Q3 An oscilloscope (CRO) can be used to show a sound wave as a **transverse** wave.

a) Mark the **wavelength** and the **amplitude** of the wave on the diagram.

b) i) What does the **amplitude** of a wave tell you?

....

....

ii) If a sound wave has a small amplitude, will it sound loud or quiet? ....

c) Does the amplitude of an **ultrasound** wave affect how loud it sounds to a human being? Explain your answer.

....

....

Ultrasound Treatments and Scans

Q4   **Ultrasound** can be used to monitor the growth of a foetus.

Complete the following using words from the list.

foetus	reflected	media	detected	echoes	body	image

Ultrasound waves can pass through most parts of the ....

Whenever an ultrasound wave reaches the boundary between two different

................................, some of the wave is .... back and can

be .... These .... can be processed by a

computer to give an .... of the ....

Q5   A concentrated beam of **ultrasound** can be used to treat kidney stones.

a)   What is ultrasound?

....

b)   What effect does the ultrasound beam have on kidney stones?

....

c)   Give two reasons why using ultrasound is a good way of treating kidney stones.

1...

2...

Q6   Ultrasound can be used in a similar way to **X-rays**.

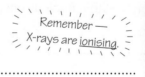

Remember —
X-rays are <u>ionising</u>.

a)   Why is ultrasound **safer** than X-rays?

....

b)   State whether X-rays or ultrasound would be used to
investigate a suspected **broken bone**, and explain why.

....

....

<u>Top Tips:</u>   Amazing really that you can learn so much using sound waves. The main thing
to remember is that ultrasound is safe and extremely useful. You might be asked to explain how
ultrasound is used in body scans and for removing kidney stones — so make sure you know.

Radioactive Decay

Q1   Write down the **atomic** number and **mass** number for each type of radiation.

   a) **alpha**   atomic number = ... mass number = ...

   b) **beta**   atomic number = ... mass number = ...

   c) **gamma**   atomic number = ... mass number = ...

Q2   Complete the table below by choosing the correct word from each column.

Radiation Type	Charge positive/none/negative	Relative mass no mass/small/large	Relative speed slow/fast/very fast
alpha			
beta			
gamma			

Q3   Complete the passage using words from the list.

chemical   random   decay   radiation   nucleus   element   temperature

Radioactive .... is a totally .... process. At some

point an unstable .... will decay and emit ....

What is left behind is often a new .... There is nothing that can

make an unstable nucleus decay. It is unaffected by .... or

.... bonding.

Q4   The diagram shows uranium-238 decaying into thorium by **alpha** emission.

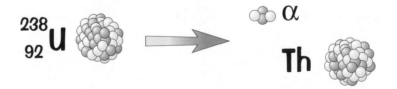

$$^{238}_{92}U \longrightarrow \quad \alpha \quad Th$$

Write the full **nuclear equation** for this decay, clearly showing the atomic and mass numbers.

....

Radioactive Decay

Q5 When a nucleus emits an **alpha** or **beta** particle, the nucleus **changes**.

  a) What happens to a nucleus when it emits an **alpha particle**?

  ....

  ....

  ....

  b) What happens to a nucleus when it emits a **beta particle**?

  ....

  ....

  ....

Q6 Explain **clearly** why:

  a) a radium atom, $^{226}_{88}$Ra, turns into a radon atom, $^{222}_{86}$Rn, when it emits an alpha particle.

  ....

  ....

  b) a carbon atom, $^{14}_{6}$C, turns into a nitrogen atom, $^{14}_{7}$N, when it emits a beta particle.

  ....

  ....

Q7 When radioactive decay occurs, radiation is emitted and **new elements** may be formed.

  a) Write a nuclear equation to show thorium, $^{234}_{90}$Th, decaying to form protactinium, $^{234}_{91}$Pa.

  ....

  b) Write a nuclear equation to show radon, $^{222}_{86}$Rn, decaying by **alpha** emission to polonium, Po.

  ....

  c) Write a nuclear equation to show nickel, $^{60}_{28}$Ni, being formed by the **beta** emission of cobalt, Co.

  ....

Top Tips: Put 'nuclear' in front of anything and it sounds extra scary*. Fortunately, nuclear equations aren't nearly as scary as they sound. Learn the atomic numbers and mass numbers for each type of radiation and you'll be well on the way to equation bliss. After a bit of practice you'll find that balancing the equations isn't that bad — just a bit of adding and subtracting. *except the word sheep

Radioactivity and Half-Life

Q1   Tick the boxes to show whether the following statements are true or false.

                                                            True **False**

  a)   The number of radioactive nuclei in a sample always stays the same. ☐ ☐

  b)   Radioactive materials decay at different rates. ☐ ☐

Q2   Complete the passage using **some** of the words given below.

long	photo	time	all	half	ionise	atoms	gamma
alpha	beta	short	increases	decreases	decay		

The radioactivity of a sample always .... over time. Each time a decay

happens ...., ... or .... radiation is emitted.

The half-life is the .... taken for .... of the unstable

.... now present to .... An isotope with a ....

half-life decays more quickly than an isotope with a .... half-life.

Q3   The half-life of uranium-238 is **4500 million years**. The half-life of carbon-14 is **5730 years**.

  a)   What do the '**238**' in "uranium-238" and the '**14**' in "carbon-14" mean?

    ....

    ....

  b)   If you start with a sample of each element and the two samples
have equal activity, which will lose its radioactivity more **quickly**?
Circle the correct answer.

        uranium-238   **carbon-14**

Q4   The half-life of strontium-90 is **29 years**.

  a)   What will have happened to a pure sample of strontium-90 in 29 years' time?

    ....

  b)   If you start with **1000** nuclei of strontium-90, how many
would you expect there to be left after **87 years**?

    ....

Q5   The activity of a radioisotope is **960 Bq**. 1 hour later, the activity has dropped to **15 Bq**.
What is the source's half-life? Tick the correct box.

    ☐ 15 mins   ☐ 10 mins   ☐ 12 mins   ☐ 3 mins

Radioactivity and Half-Life

Q6 The graph shows how the **activity** of a radioactive isotope **declines with time**.

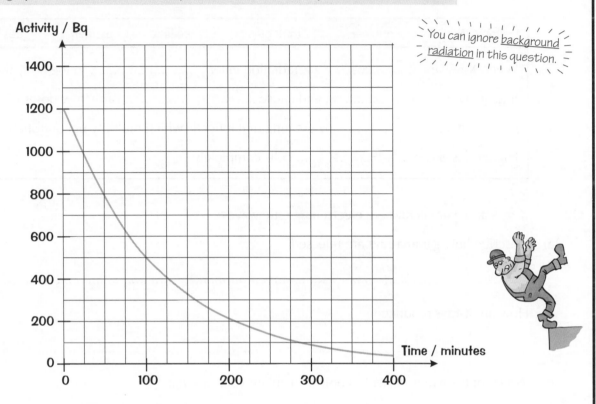

You can ignore background radiation in this question.

a) After how long was the activity down to 100 Bq? ....

b) Estimate the **half-life** of this isotope ....

c) What was the activity after 3 half-lives? ....

d) What fraction of the original radioactive nuclei will still be unstable after 5 half-lives?

....

Q7 A radioactive isotope has a half-life of **40 seconds**.

a) What **fraction** of the original unstable nuclei will still be present after 6 minutes?

....

....

b) i) If the **initial** activity of the sample was **8000 Bq**, what would be the activity after 6 minutes?

....

....

ii) After how many **whole minutes** would the activity have fallen below 10 Bq?

....

....

Ionising Radiation

Q1   Use the words in the list below to complete the paragraph.

ionisation	nuclear	molecules	cells	cancer	destroy

When X-ray and .... radiation enter .... in the body they may

interact with .... and cause .... Fairly low doses of radiation

can cause ...., by creating mutant cells which multiply uncontrollably.

Higher doses can .... cells completely.

Q2   X-rays and gamma rays are **electromagnetic waves**.

a)   Describe how **gamma rays** are released.

....

b)   How are **X-rays** produced?

....

c)   Which of the two is easier to **control**? Explain your answer.

....

Q3   The three different types of nuclear radiation can all be **dangerous**.

a)   Which **two** types of radiation can pass into the human body from outside?
Circle the correct answers.

    alpha   beta   gamma

b)   **i)** Which type of nuclear radiation is usually
most dangerous if it's **inhaled** or **swallowed**? ....

ii) Describe the **effects** this type of radiation can have on the human body.

....

....

Q4   Alpha particles can cause **ionisation** of atoms.

a)   Circle the correct word to complete this statement:

Alpha particles remove electrons from atoms leaving the atoms **negatively** / **positively** charged.

b)   Give two reasons why alpha particles are good at ionising atoms.

1. ....

2. ....

Medical Uses of Radiation

Q1   Complete the following paragraph on **radiotherapy** using the words provided.

ill   centre   normal   kill   cells   focused   cancer   rotating   radiotherapy

High doses of gamma radiation will .... living ....

Because of this, gamma radiation is used to treat .... This is called

.... Gamma rays are .... on the tumour using a wide beam.

Damage to .... cells can make the patient feel very ....

This damage is minimised by .... the radioactive source around the body,

keeping the tumour at the ....

Q2   Iodine-123 is commonly used as a **tracer** in medicine.

a) Normal iodine has a mass number of 127. Why is it no good as a tracer?

....

b) The thyroid gland normally **absorbs** iodine.
Describe how iodine-123 can be used to detect whether the thyroid gland is **working properly**.

....

....

....

c) Give **one** reason, other than safety, why alpha emitters cannot be used as tracers.

....

Q3   The table shows the **properties** of **four** radioisotopes.

Radioisotope	Half-life	Type of emission
technetium-99m	6 hours	gamma
phosphorus-32	14 days	beta
cobalt-60	5 years	beta/gamma
radium-226	1600 years	alpha

a) Which radioisotope would be best to use as a **medical tracer** and why?

....

....

....

b) Which radioisotope would a hospital use to **treat cancer** patients? Explain your answer.

....

....

Uses of Radiation and Background Radiation

Q1 Which of the following are **true**? Circle the appropriate letter(s).

    A   A large proportion of the UK's background radiation comes from natural sources.

    B   The nuclear industry produces most of the background radiation in the UK.

    C   If there were no radioactive substances on Earth, there would be no background radiation.

Q2 A radioactive source is used in **smoke detectors**.

Briefly describe how a smoke detector works.

....

....

....

....

....

Q3 Dimoilco knows that its pipeline is **leaking** somewhere between points B and D.
To find the leak, they plan to inject a source of radiation into the pipeline, then pass
a sensor along the surface above the pipeline to detect where radiation is escaping.

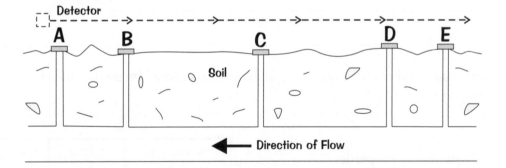

    a)   **i)** What **type** of radioactive source should they inject? Circle the correct answer:

                       alpha   **beta**   **gamma**

       ii) Give a reason for your answer to part **i)**.

....

....

    b)   At which **point** (A-E) should they inject the radioactive material? Explain your answer.

....

....

Radioactive Dating

Q1 Carbon-14 makes up **1/10 000 000** of the carbon in the air.

Living animals take in carbon-14 from the air.

a) Name one gas in the air which contains **carbon**.

....

b) What **proportion** of the carbon present in organisms alive now is carbon-14?

....

c) What happens to the level of carbon-14 in a plant or animal after it **dies**?

....

Q2 An ancient wooden spoon was found to have 1 part carbon-14 to 80 000 000 parts carbon. Work out when the wood was **living material**. (The half-life of carbon-14 is 5730 years.)

....

....

....

Q3 Uranium-238 has a half-life of **4.5 billion years**.

Rock, 243 019 yrs,
but young at heart.
Cumbria based, GSOH.
Likes: the outdoors.
Dislikes: dogs, moss

a) Explain how the decay of uranium can be used to **date rocks**.

....

....

b) The Earth is around 4.5 billion years old. How much of the Earth's **original** uranium-238 is left?

....

c) A meteorite contains uranium-238 and lead in a **ratio of 1:3**. How old is the meteorite?

....

....

Top Tips: Remember, there's two ways you can use radioactive materials to date stuff, the amount of carbon-14 left in things that were once alive, and the ratio of uranium-238 to lead in rocks. The smaller the amount of carbon-14 or uranium-238, the older things are. Maybe one day, a few thousand years in the future, someone will dig up your dead hamster and date it using carbon-14.

Nuclear Power

Q1 Choose from the following words to complete the passage.

split	chemical	turbine	electricity	uranium	water
wine	steam	moped	generator	reactors	heat

Inside a nuclear reactor, ... or plutonium atoms ....

and release .... energy. This energy is used to turn ....

into .... The steam then turns a ...., which in turn

drives a ...., producing ....

Q2 In a nuclear reactor a controlled fission **chain reaction** takes place.

a) Describe a fission **chain reaction**, starting with
a single uranium nucleus absorbing a **slow-moving neutron**.

....

....

....

....

b) Write a nuclear equation for an atom of uranium-235 **absorbing a neutron**.

....

c) What type of device uses an **uncontrolled** fission chain reaction?

....

Q3 Nuclear reactors have **control rods**, which are usually made of boron.

Think about what boron is good at <u>*absorbing*</u>.

a) How do these **boron** rods control the reaction?

....

b) What would happen if there were **no** control rods (or other control mechanism) in the reactor?

....

c) What would happen if there were **too many** control rods in the reactor?

....

Module P4 — Radiation for Life

Nuclear Power

Q4   The diagram shows a gas-cooled **nuclear reactor**.

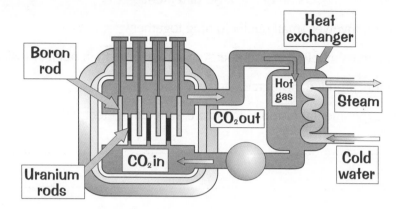

a) Why do there have to be **free neutrons** in the reactor to start it up?

....

b) Describe how **heat** is generated in the reactor.

....

....

c) What is the function of the **carbon dioxide** (CO_2)?

....

d) Why is the reactor surrounded with a very thick layer of **concrete**?

....

Q5   Uranium-236 is an **unstable** isotope of uranium.

a) Describe how uranium-236 is **formed** inside a nuclear reactor.

....

b) U-236 decays to form **two neutrons** and **two new elements**: krypton-90 and barium-144.
Write the nuclear equation for this decay. (Atomic numbers Kr = 36, Ba = 56, U = 92.)

....

Top Tips: The key thing with nuclear power is to remember what goes on in the reactor. It's really just one big nuclear kettle. A controlled chain reaction is set up and releases heat, which is used to heat water and produce steam. After that it's just like almost all power stations — the steam turns a turbine which turns a generator which makes electricity, which makes cups of tea galore.

Nuclear Fusion

Q1   Tick the boxes to show whether the following statements are **true** or **false**.
Write out the correct version of any false statements.

True   False

a)   Nuclear fusion involves small nuclei joining together.

b)   For the same mass, nuclear fission releases more energy than nuclear fusion.

c)   Fusion reactors produce lots of radioactive waste.

d)   Only a few experimental fusion reactors are generating electricity.

....

....

....

Q2   Nuclear fusion releases **energy**.

a)   Write down a nuclear equation of the fusion reaction between two different isotopes of **hydrogen**.

....

b)   **i)** Write down **two conditions** needed for nuclear fusion to take place.

1. ....   2. ....

ii) Explain why these conditions make fusion reactors extremely **hard to build**.

....

....

c)   List three things that are **shared** by international groups carrying out fusion power research.

1. ....   2. ....   3. ....

Q3   In 1989, two scientists claimed to have created energy through **cold fusion**.

a)   In what ways did they say cold fusion was **different** from previous ideas about nuclear fusion?

....

b)   Why were the cold fusion data and experiments **shared** with other scientists?

....

c)   Explain why some scientists **accepted** the idea of cold fusion whilst others didn't.

....

....

Mixed Questions — Module P4

Q1 The diagram shows an aircraft being **refuelled**. No safety precautions have been taken.

a) i) Explain how **static electricity** could cause an **explosion** in this situation.

....

....

ii) Give one **precaution** that can be taken to avoid this danger.

....

b) The aircraft needs a new lick of **paint**. Describe how static electricity could be used to make sure that an **even coat** of paint is sprayed onto the aircraft.

....

....

Q2 Radioactive tracers are important in **medicine** and **industry**.

a) Explain what is meant by the word '**tracer**'.

....

b) Give **two** reasons why an **alpha** source would not be suitable to use as a **medical** tracer.

....

....

c) Give **one** example of how tracers are used in **industry**.

....

Q3 The diagram below shows part of a **chain reaction**.

a) What is the name of the **radioactive process** shown in the diagram? ....

b) This process is part of a **chain reaction**. Describe what happens in this chain reaction.

....

....

Mixed Questions — Module P4

Q4 Paul wants to set the mood for his date with some romantic lighting.
He dims the lights using a **dimmer** switch which works as a **variable resistor**.

I can still see your face...

a) Describe how the dimmer switch **dims** the lights.

....

....

Position	Resistance (Ω)	Current (A)
1	50	
2		2.3
3		9.2

b) Because he's such a charmer, Paul entertains his date by taking some **current** and **resistance** readings with the dimmer switch in three different positions. The voltage is 230 V. Complete the table.

c) In which position will the lights be **brightest**? ....

d) Paul buys his date a lamp as a gift, but it doesn't come with a **fuse**.

i) The lamp has a power rating of **60 W**. How much current will it draw from a 230 V supply?

....

ii) Paul has fuses rated at **3 A**, **5 A** and **13 A**. Which one should he use in the lamp? ....

iii) Explain how fuses help prevent electric **shocks**.

....

....

Q5 Fay measures the **activity** of a sample of copper-64. The graph below shows her results.

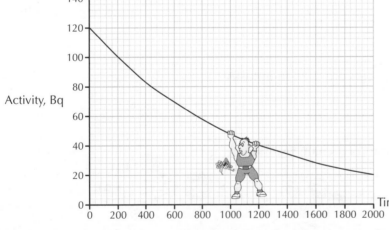

a) Find the **half-life** of copper-64. Give your answer in hours.

....

....

....

....

b) Fay is worried that background radiation might affect her readings.

i) Give a **source** of background radiation.

....

ii) Give one reason why background radiation **changes** from place to place.

....

Module P4 — Radiation for Life